Synergy
THE ULTIMATE CELL GUIDE

Phil Green

kevin
mayhew

First published in 2002 by KEVIN MAYHEW LTD
Buxhall, Stowmarket, Suffolk, IP14 3BW
E-mail: info@kevinmayhewltd.com

© 2002 Phil Green

The right of Phil Green to be identified as the author of this work
has been asserted by him in accordance with the Copyright, Designs
and Patents Act, 1988.

No part of this publication may be reproduced, stored in a retrieval system, or transmitted,
in any form or by any means, electronic, mechanical, photocopying, recording or otherwise,
without the prior written permission of the publisher.

All rights reserved.

Scripture quotations are taken from the Holy Bible,
New International Version. Copyright © 1973, 1978, 1984,
by International Bible Society. Used by permission of
Hodder & Stoughton Limited. All rights reserved.

Acknowledgements for book quotations:
James Montgomery Boice, *Ordinary Men Called By God* © 1998 by James Montgomery Boice. Published by Kregel Publications, Grand Rapids, MI, USA. Used by permission. All rights reserved.
D. A. Carson, *The Sermon on the Mount,* Paternoster Press, 1998 © D. A. Carson. Used by permission of Baker Book House, PO Box 6287, Grand Rapids, MI 49516-6287, USA.
Richard Foster, *Celebration of Discipline,* Hodder & Stoughton, 1989. © Richard Foster. Reproduced by permission of Hodder & Stoughton Limited, 338 Euston Road, London NW1 3BH.
Richard Foster, *Money, Sex and Power,* Hodder & Stoughton, 1985. © Richard Foster. Reproduced by permission of Hodder & Stoughton Limited, 338 Euston Road, London NW1 3BH.
Bill Hybels and Mark Mittelberg, *Becoming a Contagious Christian,* Copyright © 1994 by Bill Hybels and Mark Mittelberg. Used by permission of Zondervan, 5300 Patterson Avenue SE, Grand Rapids, MI 49530, USA.
R. C. H. Lenski, *The Interpretation of St Matthew's Gospel,* Augsburg, 1964. © R. C. H. Lenski. Used by permission of Augsburg Fortress Publishers, PO Box 1209, Minneapolis, MN 55440-1209, USA.
Dr D. Martin Lloyd-Jones, *Studies in the Sermon on the Mount,* Inter-Varsity Press, 1977. © D. Martin Lloyd-Jones. Used by permission of Inter-Varsity Press, 38 De Montfort Street, Leicester, LE1 7GP.
John R. W. Stott, *The Message of the Sermon on the Mount,* Inter-Varsity Press, 1984. © John Stott. Used by permission of Inter-Varsity Press, 38 De Montfort Street, Leicester, LE1 7GP.

9 8 7 6 5 4 3 2 1 0

ISBN 1 84003 997 3
Catalogue No. 1500555

Cover design by Angela Selfe
Edited and typeset by Elisabeth Bates
Printed and bound in Great Britain

Contents

Introduction	5
Introduction to cell group	7
The Welcome Section	13
The Worship Section	25
The Witness Section	39
Word Series 1 – Back to Basics	49
Word Series 2 – Blueprint for Life	71
Word Series 3 – Character Reference	129
Word Series 4 – Jesus	151

Introduction

Welcome to *Synergy – The Ultimate Cell Group Guide*. This is a resource packed full of material and ideas for you to use as you lead your cell group. *Synergy* was originally written for school cell groups, however the ideas in this guide are extremely flexible and can be used in many different contexts, making *Synergy* an essential resource for all small group leaders. The aim of the material is to give you ideas that you can adapt for your own setting, therefore *Synergy* is very versatile – tried and tested with groups of all ages.

The dictionary definition of synergy is: The interaction or co-operation of two or more agents, organisations, people etc., to produce a new or enhanced effect compared to their separate effects. (Greek *sunergos* 'working together'.) This is the thinking behind the title of the cell guide. *Synergy* contains ideas from many different people and many more have been involved in its production. I have tried to accredit these people wherever possible, however, I apologise now for any I might have missed out.

I would especially like to thank Scott Carr, Tim Cooper, Neil Fox, Ian France and David Pepper of Ipswich Christian Youth Ministries for their help and support during the production of *Synergy*. Whether it was ideas, prayer support, commenting on the drafts or dealing with the financial side of things, their help was very much appreciated and essential to the publication. I would also like to thank Susan Green (my mum) and Rebekah Green (my wife) for their support and the hours they have spent proof-reading the countless number of drafts.

I hope you find this guide useful and that it helps you and your cell group go deeper with God. I pray that you will see your cell group grow, as your friends become Christians.

Introduction to cell group

The four Ws

Traditionally a cell group meeting has the famous four Ws structure; these are Welcome, Worship, Word and Witness. The idea of this simple, but flexible structure is to make cell groups easier to plan and to make sure that everything is included in the meeting. However, it needs to be remembered that, as with any structure, it is flexible; it is there to help you, not hinder you. This guide contains hundreds of ideas for the 'Welcome', 'Worship' and 'Witness' section of your cell group meeting, along with four complete series you can use for the 'Word' section.

The aims of a cell group

In Matthew 22:34-40, Jesus is asked what the greatest commandment is. He replies:

'Love the Lord your God with all your heart and with all your soul and with all your mind.' This is the first and greatest commandment. And the second is like it: 'Love your neighbour as yourself.'

It is from these two commands given to us by Jesus that the threefold aim of cell groups is derived:

1. Love God
2. Love one another
3. Love the world

It is these three things that your cell group should be striving to achieve.

The cell values

We might not often think about it consciously but we all have values – things that are important to us. For example, some people value keeping fit so spend a lot of time at the gym and are very careful about what they eat. Cell groups have six values, these are looked at in more detail in the 'Back to Basics' section:

1. Jesus at the centre.
2. Everyone grows.
3. Everyone has a role.
4. Living the life together.
5. Multiply by reaching out.
6. Belong before you believe before you behave.

These values are not just important for cell groups, they should be held by every Christian community. The values also illustrate the bifocus of cell groups – they should be about both discipleship and evangelism.

If you are new to cell groups I suggest that you get hold of one of the many books that have been written about cell groups.

How to prepare a cell group

It is very important how you go about preparing a cell meeting. A well-planned meeting will be far more successful than something prepared five minutes beforehand.

It is often better to prepare for your cell meeting with others rather than on your own – three brains together can achieve more than three brains individually. This is actually what the word 'synergy' means. It will also enable you to support each other and share the load – being a cell group leader is not always easy. In your cell group there are likely to be either two leaders co-leading the cell, or a leader and an intern, so there should always be two people who can prepare together. It might also be possible to get your supervisor involved in the preparations some of the time. Your supervisor should be a really useful resource, so make the most of them.

My advice would be this: to meet together every week a few days before the cell meeting for at least half an hour to plan and pray, then to meet 15 minutes before the cell group meeting to finalise the programme and to pray together.

So what should you think about when you meet together and how should you go about planning for your cell group meeting?

Evaluating

A good place to start is to consider how the last cell went. It is very easy to go from one cell to another without ever evaluating what is going on. If you don't evaluate you might not spot potential problems, so you will never be able to do anything about them. Here is a list of points you should consider when evaluating your last cell:

- Who was there and who wasn't?
- How did those there interact?
- Which sections went well, which didn't and why?
- What issues came up during the cell?
- Were any issues raised that didn't get dealt with?
- Did people get anything out of the cell meeting?
- How was the cell led?
- Did you dominate too much as a leader?
- Did your cell reflect the cell values?
- Did anyone feel left out?

Once you have done this, think what needs to be addressed in future cells.

For example, is there a particular issue that you need to look at in detail? Is there a particular person who needs to be drawn out or kept quiet? Then spend some time praying about what went on in the last cell. Hand things over to God and ask him to highlight areas you need to consider while planning your next cell meeting.

Thinking about your next cell group meeting

Once you have evaluated your last cell and thought about what you need to address in the next one, you can begin to think and pray about how you are going to do this. Prayer is vital, pray that God will give you wisdom and guidance to know what to do and how to do it.

Those reading this will be in different situations: some of you will have a totally blank piece of paper – what you do in the next cell meeting is entirely up to you; while others will probably be part of a cell network and have material provided for them. However, if you are following a series, still be flexible and open to God – there is nothing wrong with having a 'week off' from the series and then coming back to it. Or it might be that you need to spend another week looking at the topic you looked at in the previous cell. Always remember that your cell supervisor should be available if you need advice on what to do.

Begin your preparation with what you thought about when you evaluated your previous cell meeting. After you have prayed about the last cell, pray that God would show you how to follow on from that. From this decide on the topic you will concentrate on in your next cell, and then work out everything else around this. One problem with the four Ws structure of cell is that it can easily become very bitty and disjointed.

We will now look at how to prepare for each section in turn.

The Welcome section

This is the first section of your meeting and is likely to set the tone for the rest of it. It will normally contain an icebreaker and you need to think what you want this to achieve. Below are some of the options:

- Help people get to know each other.
- Make people feel relaxed around each other.
- Let people get out of their system what's bothering them.
- Get people to start thinking about an issue or topic you will be looking at.
- Use it as a gauge to work out where people are at.

It might be the case that during the 'Welcome' section an issue is raised that causes you to change the direction of your cell meeting. If someone raises something important, concentrate on that rather than on what you have planned. It is important that you put people first, not plans. If someone has just shared something that is causing them a lot of concern it might well be insensitive to carry on with the 'Worship' or 'Word' section; it might be far more appropriate to stop, talk about their problems and pray about it. However, a point of caution – some people might always try to pull the cell group off course by dwelling on their problems, so be aware and act appropriately.

The Worship section

The 'Worship' section is hard to plan, as it is often difficult to come up with original ideas that are non-cringeworthy. When deciding what to do, you will need to consider carefully the people in your cell. You don't want to scare people, including any non-Christians who may be there. The sections need to move people on with God and take away any preconceived ideas that the church has given them about worship. Many people, especially outside the church, see worship as just singing songs – the deeper meaning of worship is often lost.

The 'Worship' section in *Synergy* has many creative ideas on how you can worship God as a cell group, but all of these need to be taken and adapted so they are appropriate for the people in your group.

You must decide whether to have the 'Worship' section before or after the 'Word' section. It might be appropriate to use 'Worship' to prepare people for the 'Word', or to use it after the 'Word' for reflection. Sometimes it might be better to have them independent of each other.

The Word section

It is fair to say that this section of your cell meeting probably will take the most preparation. We will look at it in two parts. First we will look at preparing for the 'Word' section if you are using prepared material, such as that found in *Synergy*. Then we'll consider writing your own material from scratch.

Using material

If you use cell material it is often easy not to do any preparation and just take the cell outlines into your cell meeting and use. This is not a good idea. Cell material is rarely written to be used like this and the material in *Synergy* certainly isn't.

You need to work through the material yourselves, read through all the Bible verses and look at the questions. You then need to consider how to adapt the material to make it appropriate to your group. This is especially true if there are non-Christians in your cell group, as most cell material seems to be written with a Christian group in mind.

Some cell material has a very clear idea that it's trying to bring home so it might be necessary to expand on this and look at a wider issue – especially if it is difficult to keep your group talking. However, some cell material covers large topics and it might be necessary to narrow down the topic to fit into your cell meeting time, or it might be appropriate to split one week's cell meeting up and cover it over a number of weeks.

Preparing your own 'Word' section

It is often hard to know where to begin when you write your own 'Word' section. I'd advise that you begin with prayer, asking God to guide you about what he wants you to cover and how he wants you to cover it. After that there are probably two main ways of going about it: either decide on an issue or decide on a passage of Scripture.

Issue: If you decide on an issue then set about looking for scripture passages that look at it (use a concordance to help you). When using the Bible in this way, make sure that you never take the passage you are looking at out of context and make sure you stay true to the message of the passage, and not manipulate the passage to make it say what you want it to say. Once you have done that, think about questions you can ask to get the group discussing the various points. Remember to keep focused and design the questions so the discussion doesn't drift too much.

Passage: Spend some time reading and meditating on the passage. Then decide the main issues addressed in the passage and which ones you want to focus on in your cell. It might be appropriate to find other Bible passages that look at the same issues. Then come up with questions and pointers to get your group talking. For a more established group don't be afraid simply to ask questions such as 'What can we learn from this passage?' and then let the discussion flow, with the occasional prompt from you to keep it heading in the right direction.

It's important when preparing the 'Word' section that you make it relevant to the people in your cell group and that they can relate what you're looking at to their lives. Always make sure there is an opportunity at some point during the cell for them to work out how they can put what has been discussed into practice in their own lives.

The Witness section

It is often easy not to plan the 'Witness' section. We get to the end of the cell meeting, we spend some time praying for our non-Christian friends and then go our separate ways and that's it. If you look at the 'Witness' section in *Synergy* you will soon realise, if you haven't already, this is not how it is meant to be!

As cell leaders you need to think long and hard about what you want to achieve in the 'Witness' section of your cell group and how you are going to achieve that long term. It is good to have continuity in the 'Witness' section, so you can see progress being made. Look through the 'Witness' section in *Synergy* and begin to think how you can make the witness of your cell as effective as possible.

When you meet together as leaders, discuss how the witness of your cell group is going. Evaluate the progress that is being made and check whether you are leading by example with your own personal witness.

Although it is important to have a long-term strategy for the witness of your cell week by week, you do need to be flexible, as it might depend on who comes to your cell. If non-Christians are there, you are going to have to use the section differently than if there are only Christians present. What to do in the 'Witness' section with non-Christians is looked at in the 'Witness' section of *Synergy*.

So remember the key: pray, plan, but be flexible and be open to the Holy Spirit's guiding.

Planning vs. flexibility

Although it is important that you plan your cell meeting in advance, it is equally important that you remain flexible during it. With cell you are not likely to know who's going to be there from one week to another, and who is there will affect what you do. So remember to be willing to adapt what you prepare.

Being flexible is certainly not an excuse for a lack of preparation. If you haven't prepared anything, you have nothing to be flexible with and your cell is likely to be an unstructured mess.

We must always remain open to the leading of the Holy Spirit and let God control what goes on in our cell. We must not fall into the trap of thinking that we've prepared a cell meeting so well that we don't need God's help to run it. If we begin to think and work like that things are going to go badly.

Practicalities

We have looked at evaluating, planning the four Ws and the importance of being flexible within your plans. However, to run a good cell you also need to think about some of the practical details. When you meet together as leaders you need to make sure that these things are sorted and if necessary communicated to the rest of your cell. Below are some of the practicalities you need to think about before you run a cell group meeting.

- Where and when are you going to meet?
- Does everyone in the group know this and can everyone get there?
- How do you want the room set up?
- Are you going to have refreshments? If so, who's going to be sorting them out?
- Have you got access to any equipment you might need? For example, CD Player, paper and pens.
- Who's going to lead each section?
- Do you need to finish at a set time?
- How are people going to get home afterwards?

Conclusion

There is no 'set in stone' method for planning a cell group meeting, but I hope that this has given you some ideas that will help you as you lead your cell group. What is important is that God uses your cell group to change lives. You and the others you lead will need to come up with a method of planning that suits you and keeps Jesus at the centre.

The Welcome Section
A few years' supply of icebreakers

Ideas from Laura Barber, Michelle Bond, Tim Cooper, Emma Cordle, Scott Carr, Laura Fell, Neil Fox, Angela Freed, Jo Furey, Phil Green, Fiona Mackay, Rebekah Green, Gavin Stone and Andrew Wright.

Introduction – What's the point of an icebreaker?

The Welcome section of a cell normally contains an icebreaker, but the question has to be asked: Why do we always start a cell group with an icebreaker? Is there really any point?

Well, the answer is a big YES!

The idea of an icebreaker is to make everyone feel comfortable with each other. The idea of a cell is that everybody shares. To do this everyone needs to be able to feel comfortable about talking in the group. By doing an icebreaker people should feel more at ease about this. However, that's not the only reason for doing one. An icebreaker is a multi-purpose tool. It can make people think about a certain theme. It can make them laugh, it can help them find out about each other and much more.

Hopefully, by now you have an idea how important the Welcome section is. However, that doesn't solve the main problem, that is, thinking up that icebreaker five minutes before the cell is about to start!! If you have that problem, you're going to love the next few pages because they're jam-packed with nothing else other than icebreakers. They're even ordered into categories so you can find the right icebreaker for every occasion.

Getting to know each other

- Get everyone to find out three things about another person in the group (the weirder the better!).

- Get everyone to find out as much as possible about a partner, then tell the rest of the group about them.

- Get everyone to find out as many things as possible that you have in common with the person sitting next to you.

- Get the members of your group to act out or draw what they do (i.e. school/job and/or hobbies).

- Get everyone to write down three things about themselves on a piece of paper. Then collect the pieces of paper up and read them out to the rest of the group. See if they can guess whose bit of paper it is.

- Get everyone to draw a timeline in the middle of a sheet of paper from the time they were born to the present day. Get them to write in the main events of their life. They could write the good things in the top half of the paper and the bad things in the bottom half. After everyone has finished this, go round and get everyone to share their timeline.

- Go round the group finding out everyone's full name and what it means.

- Ask everyone in your group whether they have got/had any nicknames.

- Line up enough chairs for each person in your group. Get everyone to stand on a chair. Then get everyone to stand in height/age/month of birth/ alphabetical order, without falling off the chair or touching the walls or ceiling.

- Ask this question: If you were a chocolate bar what would you be and why?

- Get everyone to make up a rhyme about themselves, for example, 'My name's Bob and I'm a fat slob'. Go round the group and everyone has to repeat all the previous rhymes adding their own on the end.

- Get everyone to share when and how they became a Christian. (Before you use this one you need to know that everyone in your group *is* a Christian.)

Icebreakers to make you think

- Get everyone to think of an object they come across between the time when they get out of bed and go to school/work. Once everyone has thought of an object, ask them how that object reminds them of God.

- Get everyone to describe their perfect partner as a domestic appliance.

- Get everyone to draw a symbol/logo which (to them) represents God.

The following questions could be used:

- If your house burnt down tonight, which three items would you take with you?

- If you had to survive on a desert island for one year, other than necessities such as food, which two things would you want?

- What animal would you most like to be and why?

- If you could be a fictional character from any play/novel/film, who would you be and why?

- Who do you turn to when things get tough (besides God)?

- Which of the following restrictions could you tolerate better: leaving the country permanently, or, never leaving your home country?

- If you had three wishes, what would they be?
- If you wrote an autobiography, what would the title be?
- If you had to name a pub, what would you name it and why?
- If you knew that tomorrow was your last day on earth, how would you spend it?
- If you were given £1000, what would you spend it on?
- Where would you most like to be a fly on the wall?
- If you could ask God one question, what would it be?
- What do you look for in a friend?
- If you could be a part of a computer, which piece would you be and why?
- What animal would you most like to be and why?
- What is your favourite fruit and if you had to rename it, what would you call it?
- What news item has most impacted on you over the last month and why?
- If you could appear on any TV programme you liked, which one would you choose?
- In your perfect cell, what would the icebreaker be? (After everyone has said theirs go round the group and get everyone to do the icebreaker they said!)
- If you were to start up a shop, what type of shop would it be and why?
- If you were a tool, what would you be?
- If you could solve one problem in the world, which one would you solve?
- If you had to choose 10 objects to fit in a normal size suitcase to represent life at the beginning of the new millennium, what would you choose and why?
- How would you spend your perfect day? (Include things like, what time you would get up, what you would do, who you would see and what you would eat.)

The good old days

The following questions could be used:

- What were your most favourite children's TV programmes when you were young?
- What was your most favourite childhood toy?
- What was your most favourite childhood story?

- What is your earliest childhood memory?
- What was your favourite Sunday school song?
- What were you most scared of as a child?

Revealing icebreakers

- Get each person in your group to complete the following statement: 'People might be surprised to learn that I . . .'.
- Get everyone to bring in embarrassing photos of themselves and others in the group, or photos of when they were younger.
- Get everyone in the group to name three items they have in their bedroom which no one else in the group has.
- Play 'I have never . . .'. For this game set up enough chairs in a circle for everyone in the group except for one person. This person has to say something which they have never done. All those who have done that thing have to get up and go to a different chair. The person standing has to try and sit in one of the chairs before someone else does. The person left standing has to say something which they have never done.
- Get everyone to share the strangest dream they've ever had.

The following questions could be used:
- What is your pet peeve?
- What's your most disgusting/annoying habit?
- What is the saddest thing you've done recently?
- What was your most embarrassing moment?
- What was the worst (naughtiest) thing you ever did at school?
- Have you ever skived off school? Why? Did you get caught?
- What are you most afraid of?
- What's your worst/saddest item of clothing?
- What is the saddest tape/CD/record in your music collection?
- What was the shortest-lived good idea/phase you've ever had?
- How long was your longest ever phone call? Who was it to, what was it about and who paid the bill?

Food-related icebreakers

- Play 'Chubby Bunnies'. This is where you have to see how many marshmallows you can have in your mouth and still be able to say 'Chubby Bunnies'.

- See who can balance the most biscuits on their forehead.

- Give everyone an 'After dinner' mint. Then get each person to balance it on their forehead. Without using their hands (get them to hold their hands behind their back), they have to eat the mint.

- Place in the middle of the group a bar of chocolate, a knife, a fork, a pair of gloves and a hat. Pass round the group a tray and a die. When someone rolls a six they have to put on the hat and gloves and eat as much chocolate as possible (only using the knife and fork) until someone else rolls a six.

- See which person in your group can eat the most dry cracker biscuits in 60 seconds.

- Fill a small mixing bowl with flour, turn it over and remove the bowl and place a sweet on the top of it in the middle. Then, in turn, get people to cut a slice of 'flour cake' and remove it. The person who knocks the sweet from its place has to retrieve it – with their mouth.

- Get everyone in the group to eat a banana without using their hands.

- Pass around a selection or box of chocolates. Get everyone to pick one chocolate and describe why they are like that chocolate. Then let them eat the chocolate!

- Ask everyone, 'How do you eat your Creme Egg?' Once everyone in the group has said something give them each a Creme Egg and make them eat it that way!!

- Buy some really big, sugary doughnuts and see if anyone can eat theirs without licking their lips.

Active icebreakers

- Play Pictionary™. Divide the group into two, give each group a pen, a large sheet of paper and an envelope with things they have to draw in it. (Make sure both envelopes have the same contents.) One player from each group picks a piece of paper out of the envelope and draws what is written, without talking, miming or using symbols or words. When the group have guessed what's been drawn, someone else picks a piece of paper out of the envelope. Both groups are doing this simultaneously. Set a time limit.

- Play Bible character charades. Split the group into two teams, then get one person from one team to act out a Bible character (which they pick out of a hat), in front of their team. If their team gets it they get two points. If they don't get it within one minute, let the other team have one guess at who it is. If they get it right they get one point.

- Bible search. Tell your group a word and then they have to find a verse in the Bible where the word appears. Once you've given them a few minutes to find a verse, go round the group getting them to read the verse. You can only have each verse once, so if someone else has already read your verse and you can't find another one by the time it's your turn, you're out. You're also out if you can't find a verse. Continue this until you have a winner (if time permits!). Possible words include: sheep, donkey, camel, anoint and marriage.

- Go for a 5 to 10-minute walk. While you're walking everyone has to find out one thing they didn't already know about each member of the group.

- Split your group into threes or fours and get each small group to produce a TV advert for something silly, e.g. nose hair removal cream or dog deodorant. Present the ad to the rest of the group. (If you have a camcorder you could even record them!)

- Place lots of dried peas on a tray in the middle of the room, then give each person a straw and a pot/dish/jar. For a set amount of time each person has to transfer as many peas from the tray into the pot/dish/jar, only touching the peas with their straw.

- Killer Wink. Choose one person to go out of the room while a 'killer' is chosen. Then get the person to come back in and stand in the centre of the circle. They have to guess who the 'killer' is. The 'killer' murders someone by winking at them. The murdered individual should fall over and die. The game continues until the person has guessed who the killer is.

- Play hide 'n' seek.

- Split the group up into pairs. Then one person in each pair has to blow up a balloon and hold it with their teeth. Then go round the group putting shaving foam on all the balloons. The other person, with a razor, then has to 'shave' the balloon.

- Split your group into two teams and give them each an equal amount of newspaper and tape. Get them to make a tower that will support a mug for one minute. The tallest tower wins.

- Ask one person to choose a movement (e.g. winking or crossing their legs). The person next to them has to do that movement and one of their own; the next person does the first movement and the second and then their own and so on.

- Foot tapping game. Get two volunteers into the middle of a circle. They lock hands with each other. The aim of the game is to tap the top of one of their opponent's feet with their foot. Once one of the opponents has been 'tapped' three times, they sit down and the winner challenges someone else from the circle.

- Put a label on everyone's back with a name of a famous person on it. Other people have to give them clues as to who that famous person is.

- Take a large, empty cereal box and place it (upright) on the floor. Each group member has to pick up the box with their mouth without putting their hands, knees or elbows on the floor. After each member has done this tear a few centimetres off the top of the box. Continue until all members have failed or the 'box' is now a flat piece of cardboard.

- Make a human pyramid.

- Make and untie a human knot. To do this get everyone to stand in a circle and grab someone else's left hand with their left hand. Then grab someone else's right hand with your right hand. Without anyone letting go, untie the knot so you are left standing in a big circle all holding hands.

- Split the group into pairs. Put shaving foam on the face of one person in each pair. Then give the other person a bowl of Coco-pops™ (or equivalent) and get them to stand two metres or so away from their partner. They have to throw the Coco-pops™ into the mouth of their partner.

- Have an aerobics session.

- Get everyone to make a paper aeroplane. Get them to turn it upside down and put it on the table. Then get everyone to blow their plane along the table. First one over the finish line wins.

- Play 'pass-the-parcel' making sure you have some very interesting forfeits.

- Draw a fairly simple maze on a piece of paper and photocopy it as many times as is required. Split the cell up into pairs. One person in each pair needs to be blindfolded and given a pen. Then the other person has to talk them 'through' the maze. When deciding on the winner bear in mind both the time it took them to complete the maze and how neat the line is!

Games you can buy

All these games make excellent icebreakers and can be bought from all good toy shops!

- Jenga™
- Twister™
- Taboo™
- Pit™
- Uno™
- Dingbats™
- Card games

Finding out how people are doing

- Give everyone in your group an object. (For example, a children's toy or something out of a cracker.) Ask them one, or some, of the following questions:

    How does this object relate to how you feel at the moment?
    How does this object relate to what you think about God/the Bible?
    How does this object relate to what your expectations of cell are today?

    (You could give everyone a different object at the end of the cell and ask them: How does this object relate to how you thought cell went today? What have you got out of cell today?)

- Ask everyone to put an object/item in the middle of the group that best describes their life right now.

- Give everyone in the group a paper plate and pen or a lump of plasticine/Blu-Tack/play-doh. Ask them to draw/make a face that best describes how they are feeling at the moment.

The following questions could be used:

- What type of car best describes your Christian life at the moment? What car would you like your Christian life to be like?
- What is the coolest thing that has happened to you over the last week?
- If you could describe your life at the moment as a song, which would it be?
- What was the best thing anyone said to you this week?
- What has God taught you this week?
- What have you got to thank God for in the last week?
- Which colour best describes how you feel towards God at the moment?
- What road sign best describes how you feel at the moment?

Best, worst, happiest, saddest

The following questions could be used:

- What was the biggest waste of money in your life, ever?
- What is the worst joke you have ever heard?
- What was the best and/or worst birthday/Christmas present you have ever had?
- What was the happiest moment of your life?
- What was the best holiday you've ever been on?

- What was the biggest decision you've ever had to make?
- What is the best surprise you've ever received?
- What is the best and worst thing you've ever done to, or, for someone?
- What is the best/worst film you've ever seen?
- What is the best compliment you have ever received?
- What is your best time of day and why?
- What Christmas decoration is your favourite, and why?
- What is the best book you've ever read?
- What was the scariest/most frightening experience of your whole life?

Heroes and villains

The following questions could be used:

- As a child who did you look up to most?
- Who do you most respect?
- Who was the worst teacher you ever had and what were they like?
- Whose faith (in God) do you most admire?
- Who, in all of history, would you most like to be shipwrecked with for a year?
- Who is the one person who gets right up your nose?
- If you were going to have 'The ultimate party', who would you invite, and who wouldn't you invite and why?
- If you could be anyone for a day, who would you be?
- If you could have a one-to-one with anyone, (past, present or future) who would it be and why?

Uncategorised but good icebreakers

- Give everyone in your group a balloon and a marker pen. Get them to draw the face of the person on their left on the balloon.
- Pass an object round your group (e.g. magazine or CD), get each person, in turn, to invent an alternative use for the object. Use another object once the ideas have dried up.
- Go round the group and get everyone to complete the following about the person on their right: 'I love [*name of person*] because [*positive point, gift, talent, etc.*]'

- Have a Bible or general knowledge quiz.
- Share answers to prayer.
- Go round the group and make up a story, each person just adding one word at a time.
- You start off with a word and then the person next to you has to say another word related to it, then the next person has to say a word related to that one and so on. If someone says a word you've already had, they are out.
- The aim of this game is to count to 20 as a group. Easy, you might think, but you just try it. The rules are as follows:
  - There must be no planning or talking other than to say a number.
  - Each number must be called out once in consecutive ascending order.
  - Only one person can call out a number at a time or you have to start again.
  - Stand in a circle facing away from each other.
  - The same person cannot call out two consecutive numbers.
- Play chinese whispers. This is when one person whispers a story to the person sitting next to them, who then repeats it to their other neighbour. The last person in the group then tells you all the story. After this, the first person tells you how the story started.
- Give someone a subject (e.g. baked beans, the inside of a table tennis ball, grass) and get them to speak to the rest of the group about that subject for one minute.
- Get each member to pick out a piece of paper with a name of an object written on it. They then have to share the gospel message using the object as an illustration.
- Get everyone to write their names on the top of a piece of paper. Pass the papers round and get everyone to write something encouraging about that person.
- Nominate a 'psychiatrist' and tell them that they are going to have to guess the disorder of the patients by asking questions. Send them out of the room. Then explain to the rest of the group how they are to answer the questions. If you get asked a question by the 'psychiatrist' you answer as if you are the person sitting on your left. If you say something about the person on your left which is incorrect then the person on your left gets up and everyone has to change seats. Everyone now has the identity of the new person sitting on their left. The 'psychiatrist' has to continue diagnosing until they come up with the correct diagnosis.
- Tell the group you are about to share a dream with them that you had the other night. Then ask one person to leave the room. They will have to come in and guess what the dream was about, by asking yes/no

questions only. Once they have left the room tell the rest of the group about the dream. The problem is, you didn't have a dream the other night!! What you are going to do is answer the questions as follows:

– If the question ends in a vowel the answer will be 'yes'.

– If the question ends in a 'Y' the answer will be 'maybe'.

– If the question ends in a consonant the answer will be 'no'.

- Get everyone to write on a piece of paper their favourite colour and season of the year. Then put all the pieces of paper in a hat and pick out one each. Read out what it says and try to guess whose it is.

- Play the 'Yes'/'No' game. This is when you choose one person from the group. Then everybody has to ask them questions. The person being asked the questions must not answer any of the questions with a 'yes' or 'no'. Time them to see how long they last. Give everyone in your group a turn.

The following questions could be used:

- What do you do to relax?

- Who have you spent most time with in the past week and how much time?

- Describe your best friend/person sitting next to you as a food dish.

- If you could be in a band, which band would it be and why?

- Who is the most famous person you've ever met? Did you actually speak to them? If yes, what did you say to them and what did they say to you?

- Where do you hide?/Where do you go to get away from everybody? (Both now and/or in the past.)

The Worship Section
Ideas to connect with God creatively

Ideas from Ruth Carling, Scott Carr, Tim Cooper, Laura Fell, Neil Fox, Angela Freed, Phil Green, Fiona Mackay, Rebekah Green, Carla Taylor and Peter Tew.

Introduction

The Worship section of cell is an excellent opportunity to connect with God – to spend time with him, to talk to him, to listen to him, to thank him and to enjoy being in his presence.

Many people think that worship is just about singing songs when we're in church. Although this is part of worship, it's only a very small part. Romans 12:1 says this about worship: 'Therefore, I urge you, brothers, in view of God's mercy, to offer your bodies as living sacrifices, holy and pleasing to God – this is your spiritual act of worship.' Our whole lives should be worship to God – what we say, what we do and how we do it. Therefore, the Worship section in cell is only really a token gesture if the rest of our life doesn't match up.

So, why have a Worship section in cell if the whole of our lives should be worshipping God? Well, worship is also about connecting with God and it is important that we do this in the cell. One of the values of cell is 'Jesus at the centre' and worship brings the focus of cell to him. As you worship God together you'll find you will grow individually and as a group. People will become more open with God and each other.

In many senses the Worship section of cell is going along with the traditional definition of worship, but you don't have to worship God in traditional ways. Be creative in your worship. If you look at God's creation, we worship a very creative God, so let's be creative in our worship of him. Everyone is different and we each have our own preferences in the way we worship God. Cell is an ideal place to experiment in the ways we worship God. We live in a multimedia age, so why don't we worship God in multi-media ways?

In this section there are lots of worship ideas. There are general ideas, there are ideas for specific times of the year, there are two series of worship ideas that you might like to follow as a cell and there are 50 passages of Scripture and 15 promises suitable to use in your worship. Take these ideas, use them, adapt them, develop them, be creative and make them work for your cell group.

Worship and icebreakers

Sometimes it might be appropriate to combine the worship and icebreaker section of your cell meeting. Below are some ideas for joint icebreakers and worship.

- Go round the group and get everyone to share one thing they have to thank God for in the last week. Then as a group pray and thank God for these things.

- Get everyone to share a recent answer to prayer, then thank God for the privilege of prayer and that he does answer your prayers. (You might like to read Matthew 7:7-12.)

- Give everyone in the group a magazine or newspaper. Ask them to find a headline, picture or article that relates to how they feel about God and/or how he feels about them.

- Get everyone to think of an object they come across between the time they get out of bed and go to school/work. Once everyone has thought of an object, ask them how the object could be related to God. Then encourage people to pray about what they have said.

- Give everyone a piece of paper and a pen/pencil. Ask them to draw a symbol that to them represents God. Then get everyone to share with the rest of the group what they have drawn and why. Finish this section with a time of prayer.

- Go round the group saying words that describe God. Go through the whole alphabet. The first person says a word that describes God beginning with 'A', the next person says a word beginning with 'B' and so on. After you have gone from A to Z say a few prayers thanking God for some of the things that were mentioned.

General ideas

Here are lots of ideas you can develop, adapt or combine to use in your cell group.

- Get everyone in the group to write a letter or poem to God telling him how they feel about him. Once everyone has done this, ask people to read theirs out if they feel comfortable to do so.

- Read a passage of Scripture (50 possibilities on pages 35-36), then get people to think about it and ask God to speak to them through it. After that, you could discuss and/or pray as a whole group, smaller groups or individually about what the passage means and what God is saying to you through it.

- Rewrite a Psalm in modern day language. You could either do it as a whole group or each write one verse. Psalm 23 is a good one to use.

- Sing songs, either *a cappella*, to CDs or make use of musical talent in your group.

- Combine music, vision and word. For example, put a video on to stimulate people's sight, then with music in the background, read a Bible passage. Leave the music on while people are thinking about what's been read.

- Use the Lord's Prayer as the focus of your worship. Be creative!

- Make a collage from newspaper and magazine cuttings. Choose a theme for your collage such as 'God's power'.

- Take an offering and give the money to a good cause.

- Ask everyone to write an article on 'God'. Get people to write the article for a different newspaper/magazine. For example, *The Sun*, *The Guardian*, *Technology Today*, *The Unexplained* or *Woman's Own*. Then get everyone to read out the article they have written.

- Give everyone in the group a stone, a label and a pen. Then ask them to write something that they have to worship God for on it. Get them to stick their label on the stone. Then as a group worship God through prayer or song. Get everyone to keep their stone, so that when they're going through a rough patch they can look back at it and remember God's goodness.

- Read John 1:1-18 over music. Leave a gap between each paragraph to let people think and pray about the words. You could conclude the time with prayer or singing a song.

- (Only try if it's OK to make a lot of noise!) Put some music on really loud, get people to stand in a circle facing outwards. Then encourage everyone to cry out to God the things that are on their hearts and in their minds and how they feel about him. This can be spoken or sung. Remind people that they won't be able to hear each other so it's between them and God.

- Make up actions/or dance to a song or passage (for example the Lord's Prayer).

- Put some music on and encourage people to spend some time alone with God (perhaps you could give them a verse to meditate on). After they have done this for a while, encourage them to listen to God, then go up to, encourage and pray with each other. Don't organise any of this, just encourage people to go up to others and pray with them and say words of encouragement.

- Set up different 'stations' in the room or in different rooms (if possible). At one 'station' you could have a CD playing, in another you could have silence and in another you could have a number of objects. Perhaps at each station you could leave a different verse. Encourage people to go to as many different rooms/stations as they wish or they could spend the whole time at one station if they wish.

- Have a creative worship session. Get people to spend some time individually or in small groups doing something creative to express their worship to God. For example, writing poetry, writing a song, drawing a picture or coming up with some music or a dance. Encourage people to share back with the rest of the group what they have done.

- Get everyone to go and find their own space and spend some time with just them and God in silence.

- Go round the group each saying something you can thank God for, keep going until it is quite clear that you're never going to be able to stop!! Then pray – thanking God for everything!

- Brainstorm on a piece of paper, as many ways as possible that you can think of, of worshipping God. Then read Romans 12:1. After this pray as a group that your whole lives would be worship to God.

- Read Hebrews 11:16. Go round the group and encourage everyone to share one thing which they are looking forward to about heaven. Then pray together, thanking God for giving us a second chance and having such an excellent reward we simply don't deserve.

- Read Joshua 24:14-15. Get people to write down on a piece of paper what gets between them and God. Throw the pieces of paper into a bin. Break up into smaller groups and pray for one another, that the things you wrote down wouldn't get between you and God any more.

- Choose a word (for example 'light') and read as many verses from the Bible as possible about that word. Spend some time in silence after reading each verse so people can think/pray about it. At the end pray as a group.

- Get each person to draw a timeline of their life, marking on it the highs and lows with God. Then encourage people to feed back what their timeline looks like with the rest of the group. Then either as a whole group or smaller groups, pray with each other thanking God for the highs and thanking him that he gets you through the lows. Also pray for those who are going through a low at the moment.

- Collect lots of stones (at least enough so everyone in the group has six stones each). Get everyone to choose five stones that represent five areas of their life (for example, God, family, friends, sin and work). Then get them to place the stones on the ground in relation to one another (i.e. themselves in the middle and the others around them, the closest thing to them goes closest and if, say, friends and sin come between them and God, put the sin and friends stone between the stone that represents them and the stone that represents God). Then encourage them to lay things before God and ask God if any changes are needed. Either as a whole group or in smaller groups feed back why you've positioned the stones where you have. Ask people if they are happy where their stones are and if they're not, how they would like them to look. You could also remove the stone that you would most like to see removed, and then pray with each other that this would happen. (Develop this idea.)

- Read Galatians 5:22-23 (Fruits of the Spirit). Then, as a whole group get everyone to create a 'freeze frame' of each of the fruits using only themselves in relation to each other. For example, if illustrating love you could all hug each other, holding still for the 'snap shot'.

- Take a narrative story from the Bible, for example, the Israelites marching round the walls of Jericho, the feeding of the 5000 or Jesus healing someone. Read the story through several times. Each time you read it through encourage people to put themselves in a position of a different character. Reflect on how the character would have felt, what they would say or any questions they might have. After this discuss the thoughts people had.

- In small groups act out some of Jesus' miracles. Then get each group to show the rest of the group to see if they can guess which one they are acting. Conclude with a time of prayer thanking Jesus for how he can change people's lives.

- Make a cross out of softwood or cardboard. Get people to pin their prayer and praise requests to it and spend some time as a group praying for these requests. Have a look at the cross each week and see which prayers have been answered and to add new ones.

Here are some worship ideas for specific times of the year.

Christmas

- Choose a Christmas carol, give everyone in the group a copy of it and read it through. Then get everyone in the group to spend some time thinking about the words. Discuss what the words mean to each of you. Finish the time off by thanking God for sending his Son, through prayer and/or song (you might like to sing the carol).

- Read John 3:16-17 and 1 Peter 3:18. Spend some time thinking, then discussing what it must have been like for God to send his Son into the world. How do you think God felt? How do you think Jesus felt? Why did he do it? Conclude this section by praying or singing.

Pentecost

- Read all or some of the following passages: Acts 2:17-21; 2 Timothy 1:7; Ephesians 2:22, and/or John 14:16-17, 26-27. Spend some time discussing how you feel about God's gift of the Holy Spirit. If there are any issues that come up, pray about them. Finish by thanking God for his gift of the Holy Spirit, either through song, prayer or both.

- Give everyone in the group a piece of paper and get them to write their name on it. Then get everyone to pass their paper to the person on their left. This person has to write something at the bottom of the piece of paper about the gifts/abilities that this person brings to the group, then fold up the bottom of the paper so what they have just written is covered. Then pass this to the next person and repeat the same thing again. Keep doing this until the paper has come back to the person it started with. Get everyone to read out what is on their piece of paper (or you could swap papers so someone else reads it). Finish by praying, thanking God that he has given you all different gifts and abilities through his Holy Spirit.

Easter

- Get hold of a copy of the *Jesus* or *Jesus of Nazareth* film (or any film that shows the crucifixion scene). Read 1 Peter 2:22-25 then show the crucifixion scenes. Then either in silence or with some quiet background music get people to reflect on these things and spend some time alone with God. Round up this time with one or a few prayers.

- Make a rugged wooden cross and place it in the centre of the room, then pass round rusty, big nails. Read some parts of the crucifixion story out and have music playing in the background. Encourage people to pray out loud about what they are thinking/feeling.

- Set up different 'stations' around the room. For example, a cross (have some paper and pens by it so people can write down something they need to lay down and leave at the cross), a bowl of water (where people can wash their hands as a symbol of being cleansed) and at another station some pillows, big cushions and/or bean bags so people can relax in God's presence. You might like to have a different Bible verse at each station. You could also have different music playing at each of the stations. Encourage people to go round to all or some of these different stations spending time alone with God.

Creation

Without getting into too much debate about whether creation actually took place in seven days or if it happened through evolution, we can worship God because of it. However creation happened, God was behind it!

This is a series of worship ideas that you might like to follow in your cell group. You might want to spend a whole session on worshipping God because of his creation or you might like to take a day each cell meeting for seven weeks. These are just some ideas; if you use them as they are it is likely to be very bland. Take these ideas and build on them – BE CREATIVE. Remember to worship God and not creation.

Day 1: Light and darkness

(You might like to have quiet music playing in the background during this section)

Read Genesis 1:1-5.

- Ask people to think about what they associate with light and what they associate with darkness.
- Read John 8:12.
- Light a candle in the middle of the room and get people to think about what the verse means to them.
- Encourage people to pray either out loud, in silence, as a whole group or in smaller groups.

Day 2: Sky

- If possible go outside and lie on some grass so people can look up into the sky. Encourage people to spend time alone with God, thinking about his greatness and the vastness of his creation and love. While people are lying on the grass read a passage from the Bible every few minutes, such as Genesis 1:6-8; Psalm 103:11-12 and Matthew 11:28-30.

Day 3: Land, sea and plants

Read Genesis 1:9-13.

You could:

- Pick a variety of plants and pass them around the group getting people to smell all of them (make sure you pick nice smelling plants!).
- Read 2 Corinthians 2:15. Discuss the awesomeness of this verse. Then pray as a group, thanking God for choosing to forgive us and asking him that we will 'smell of Christ' to those around us.

or you could:

- Think about all the beauty we see around us every day. Perhaps look at photos or videos to help you. Thank God for all his creativity and ask him to help you appreciate it more and play your part in looking after his creation.

Day 4: Sun and moon

Read Genesis 1:14-19.

- Read 2 Timothy 4:2. Then say how the sun marks the seasons of the year and as Christians we go through cycles. Sometimes, we feel like it's

summer, other times it's really hard and it feels like winter, and then there are the halfway points.
- In a room/building set up four different stations, one representing each of the seasons. (Use music, visual, smell and objects to do this.) Encourage people to go to where they feel they are at. Get them to spend some time with God there; if they don't like where they are at and want to move on, encourage them to leave whatever it is which is holding them back and move on to the season where they feel God wants them to be.

Day 5: Birds and fish

Read Genesis 1:20-24.

- Get everyone to spend some time thinking about the variety and quantity of birds and fish that God created.
- Read Matthew 10:29-31 and 6:25-34 and thank God for this. Pray for those who are worried about things at the moment. You could get people to write down what they are worried about on a piece of paper then lay it before God.

Day 6: Animals and humans

Read Genesis 1:24-27.

- In smaller groups make up drama sketches to represent how God created humans in his image and how he wants to have a special relationship with us.

Day 7: Rest

Read Genesis 2:2-3.

- God knew that it was important for us to rest; he gave us a whole day to do it. However, we can become so busy we can forget all about spending time with him. Spend this worship session in silence, resting in God's presence alone. Encourage people just to get themselves right before God, ask God to strengthen them, replenish their energy and remind them to spend more time alone with God. Perhaps after reading the passage you could sing/listen to 'To be in your presence' by Noel Richards.

Characteristics of God

This is a series of worship ideas that you could use over a period of ten weeks. Each week looks at a different characteristic of God. If your cell doesn't meet for very long you could extend these Worship ideas and use them for the Word section as well.

When we worship God we often use the things God has done for us to worship him. Although there is nothing wrong with this we must remember to worship God for who he is, not just for what he does for us.

Some people will be able to relate to some characteristics of God more easily than they can others. Encourage people to be open and share how they feel about the different characteristics of God, then you'll be able to learn from each other.

God has many more characteristics than the nine we look at here. You may like to extend the series and look at some of the others.

Week 1: Brainstorm

- Introduce and explain how you are going to use the worship section of cell for the next few weeks.
- As a group, brainstorm and write down all the characteristics of God you can think of.
- Then get everyone to pick out the characteristic that means the most to them at the moment. Encourage them to share why this is with the rest of the group. Then pray as a group thanking God for who he is.

Week 2: Friend

- Get everyone to think of their best friend and write on a piece of paper why they are their friend, what they do together and why they enjoy spending time together.
- Read and discuss John 15:15. How do you feel about having God as your friend?
- Challenge people as to whether they spend enough time with God. Would you prefer to spend an hour with God or an hour with your best friend?
- Spend a few minutes in silence thinking about God as your friend.
- Pray as a group about what you have discussed and thank God for his friendship.

Week 3: Love

Read and discuss some or all of the following passages: Zephaniah 3:17; John 3:16-18; 1 John 3:1 and/or 1 John 4:9-12.

- Write as a group or as individuals a love letter, poem or song expressing how you feel about God's love, how you feel about God and/or thanking God for his love.
- Spend some time either in song or prayer thanking God for his love.

Week 4: Creator

- You could go for a walk and as you walk thank God for all his creation you see around you. If this is not practical use imagery to bring your

thoughts to God, for example, show a video that shows the greatness and beauty of God's creation.
- Read Genesis 1:27. Discuss how this verse makes people feel. Pray about the things that come up during this discussion.

Week 5: King

- Get people to imagine what it would be like to be king/queen or heirs to the throne. Then read Romans 8:17.
- We worship a God who is king, judge and ruler of the universe but, as we saw in week two, he's also our friend. Read Jeremiah 10:10. Then pray, thanking God that even though he is the King over all, he wants a personal relationship with each one of us.

Week 6: Father/Mother

- These are characteristics people often struggle with, especially if they don't have a good relationship with their earthly father/mother. Encourage people to be honest and open but also remember to be sensitive. It might be appropriate to offer to pray with those who particularly struggle with issues in this area.
- Read Isaiah 66:13, Deuteronomy 32:6b and 1 John 3:1.
- We are children of God!! However good our earthly parents are, they are only humans so they will make mistakes. God though is a perfect parent to us. On a large piece of paper brainstorm all the ways God 'parents' us.
- Pray together thanking God that we can be called 'children of God', thank God for his parenthood, also pray for those who struggle with the Father/Mother concept of God.

Week 7: Faithful

Read Deuteronomy 7:9.

- Encourage everyone in the group to share a time where God was faithful to them.
- Listen to or sing a song about God's faithfulness to us. For example, 'Faithful One' by Brian Doerksen.
- Round up with a time of prayer thanking God for his faithfulness.

Week 8: Holy

- Discuss as a group what the word 'Holy' means.
- Read Revelation 4 over music and encourage people to think about the words. Encourage them to think about the Holy God we worship and to think about heaven.
- Encourage people to share things which they were thinking about. Then finish with a few prayers.

Week 9: Ever-present

- Read Psalm 139 and spend some time in quiet thinking and meditating on it. Encourage people to be honest before God about how the passage makes them feel. Encourage people to listen to God and let him speak to them through this passage.
- Either as a whole group or smaller groups encourage people to share what they were thinking about and what God told them. Then pray together about these things.

Week 10: Forgiving

- God is a just God, a fair judge but he forgives those who ask for forgiveness.
- Read Psalm 130:1-8 and 1 Peter 3:18.
- Spend some time alone with God asking him to highlight things you need to ask forgiveness for. Perhaps you could give everyone a piece of paper and pen and encourage them to write something down where they need to ask for forgiveness. Put a bin in the middle of the room where they can put the piece of paper.
- Listen to/sing a few songs reflecting on and thanking God for his forgiveness.

50 passages for worship

There is no better place to base our worship on than the Word of God. In this section there are 50 passages which you could use in your Worship section.

1. Genesis 9:8-17 – God's promise to Noah.
2. Exodus 15:1-18 – The song of Moses.
3. Exodus 33:18-23 – God's glory.
4. Numbers 23:19 – God keeps his promises.
5. 1 Samuel 2:1-10 – Hannah's prayer.
6. 2 Samuel 22:1-4 – The Lord is our rock.
7. 1 Kings 8:23-24 – There is no God like you.
8. 1 Chronicles 16:8-36 – David's psalm of thanks.
9. Psalm 23 – The Good Shepherd.
10. Psalm 66 – Praise God for what he's done for us.
11. Psalm 136 – God's love never fails.
12. Psalm 139 – The Lord is always near.
13. Song of Songs 8:6b-7 – Love.
14. Isaiah 40:27-31 – Strength to the weary.

15. Isaiah 45:18-19 – There is only one God.
16. Isaiah 61 – The year of the Lord's favour.
17. Lamentations 3:21-24 – We can depend on God.
18. Ezekiel 34:11-16 – The Lord looks after his sheep.
19. Daniel 2:20-23 – God's power.
20. Hosea 14:4-9 – The Lord promises to forgive.
21. Micah 7:18-20 – No one is like our God.
22. Habakkuk 1:2-5 – God will turn things around.
23. Zephaniah 3:17 – The Lord sings because of you.
24. Matthew 5:1-12 – The Beatitudes.
25. Matthew 11:28-30 – Rest for the weary.
26. Luke 1:46-55 – Mary's Song.
27. John 1:1-18 – The Word becomes flesh.
28. John 3:16-18 – God loved the world so much.
29. Acts 2:17-21 – God pours out the Holy Spirit on us.
30. Romans 3:21-24 – God makes us acceptable to him.
31. Romans 4:7-8 – God blesses those he forgives.
32. 1 Corinthians 2:9 – God's plans for us.
33. 1 Corinthians 13:1-8 – Love is . . .
34. Ephesians 2:4-10 – God's mercy.
35. Philippians 2:6-11 – Christ was . . .
36. Philippians 3:7-11 – 'All I once held dear.'
37. Colossians 1:15-20 – Christ is like God.
38. 1 Timothy 2:5-6 – There is only one God.
39. 2 Timothy 2:11-13 – Being like Christ.
40. Titus 3:4-7 – What God's done for us.
41. Hebrews 12:1-3 – Throwing off what hinders us and fixing our eyes on Jesus.
42. James 4:7-10 – Come near to God.
43. 1 Peter 2:10 – We are God's people.
44. 1 Peter 2:22-25 – What Christ did for us.
45. 1 Peter 3:18 – Christ died for our sins.
46. 2 Peter 3:8-9 – The Lord is not slow in keeping his promise.
47. 1 John 3:1 – We're children of God.
48. Jude 24-25 – God can keep us from falling.
49. Revelation 4 – Worship in heaven.
50. Revelation 15:3b-4 – The Lord God Almighty.

15 promises of God

In the Bible God has made many promises and the good thing is that he keeps them. Here are 15 promises of God we can hold on to. Think of a creative way you can use them during your worship. Perhaps you could look at a few each week.

1. Joshua 1:9
2. Psalm 3:5
3. Psalm 23:1-6
4. Isaiah 40:29-31
5. Jeremiah 29:11-13
6. Matthew 7:7-8
7. Matthew 24:13
8. John 3:16
9. Romans 8:28
10. Romans 8:38, 39
11. 1 Corinthians 2:9
12. 2 Thessalonians 3:3
13. Hebrews 13:8
14. James 4:7-8
15. 1 John 3:1

The Witness Section
Multiply by reaching out

Ideas from Scott Carr, Tim Cooper, Neil Fox, Angela Freed, Phil Green and Rebekah Green.

Introduction

The Witness section in your cell is probably the last section you do at your cell meeting. Therefore, it can often be rushed and tagged on to the end. The other problem with this section is that it can be difficult to think of original ideas week in and week out.

The Witness section is very important, because you should be looking to see your cell grow and your non-Christian friends become Christians. As a cell group it is easy to become so comfortable that you don't want to bring more people in because it might spoil things. However, it is important to live out all the cell values, one of which is 'Multiply by reaching out'.

There can be a huge struggle in cells between discipleship and evangelism. How can you create a group that disciples Christians and at the same time evangelises non-Christians? I can't tell you in easy steps how you can achieve the balance, but I do believe a balance between the two is important and that the two should and can complement each other. It is something that you need to work towards achieving and requires much prayer.

So what should you do in the Witness section? Prayer is clearly an important part. We should pray for our non-Christian friends and pray for each other as we try to share the gospel with them. However, it's often easy to fall into the trap of spending all our time praying whilst never doing anything. Remember, God often calls us to be the answer to our own prayers.

The Witness section in the cell meeting is often planning and preparing for things you will be doing outside the cell. Remember cell and Christianity is not just a meeting, it's a lifestyle; cell prepares us for what we do during our everyday lives.

In this section there are a number of ideas of how to use the Witness section in cell and how to go about the Witness section outside cell. We will look at the importance of vision and strategy and also begin to tackle one of those big questions – what do you do in the Witness section if there are non-Christians in your cell?

Vision and strategy

It is important that as a cell group/cell network you think long-term. What is the vision for your cell? What is your end in mind? When you decorate a room, the sensible thing to do is have an end in mind before you start. You decide exactly how you want the room to look, then you work out how you are going to achieve that look. It helps if we adopt this approach to cell life. Take some time as a cell group and/or cell network to pray and discuss what your vision is for your cell group/network. Ask God to show you his plans and what he wants you to be doing. Some of his pointers are clear from the Bible and the cell values provide an excellent framework for the next stage.

Once you have an end in mind, it is important you work out how you are going to get there – a strategy. Cells don't just grow and multiply overnight, it requires much prayer, effort and energy. It is likely to mean going through some very tough times; that's another reason why having an end in mind is important, it gives you something to aim at, to look forward to during the hard times. It's also important to have a strategy so you stay on track during these tough times.

Your strategy should be unique to your cell group. As a cell you should talk about what your strategy is to reach your end in mind. Below is a list of some of the things you should do and consider when coming up with your strategy.

- Pray and listen to what God wants you to do.
- Read books and speak to others about their experiences and ideas.
- Think short term as well as long term – where do you want your cell to be in three weeks, three months, three years?
- What are the strengths and weaknesses of your group? (It might be good to spend some time looking at each other's gifts.)
- Who are your target group of people that you want to share the gospel with/bring to your cell?
- Who are the people you want to bring to your cell to begin with?
- How are you going to make your cell a place where non-Christians feel accepted and comfortable?
- How are you going to balance discipleship and evangelism?

Cell socials

Cell socials are an excellent tool to build a community within your cell group and help you get to know each other better. They are also great as a first step to invite non-Christians to become part of your group. It gives them a chance to meet you socially and (hopefully!) find out that you are actually normal human beings!

There are many points you need to think about before putting on a cell social and it takes quite a lot of planning to make it successful. It might be

THE WITNESS SECTION

appropriate to consider organising an inter-cell social with the other cells in your network. Below is a list of 10 possibilities for a cell social, then there is an 11-step guide to putting on a successful cell social.

9 possible cell socials

1. Watch a video in someone's home – make sure the video you watch is appropriate.

2. Watch a film at the cinema – normally a very successful cell social. However, make sure you go out somewhere afterwards, e.g. McDonald's or pub (depending on the age of those there) as the whole idea of a cell social is so you can talk and get to know each other! Watching a film is an excellent conversation starter. Again, make sure what you watch is appropriate.

3. Go ten-pin bowling, karting, ice skating or roller skating.

4. Go out for a meal or cook a meal at someone's home. Organise a trip to the beach, local tourist attraction, theme park, concert or different town/city.

5. Invite everyone round to someone's house (or another convenient venue) to watch a sporting event on TV – you might even consider hiring or borrowing a video projector.

6. Do something you know all your friends like doing – for example, if all your cell likes playing football and all your friends like playing football, organise a football match.

7. Organise a party.

8. A games evening – computer games, murder mystery evening, Monopoly™ – just be creative.

9. Chip-shop challenge – in several cars, drive to as many different chip shops as you can, buying a portion of chips from each shop, decide which shop has the best chips and which shop has the worst chips. All meet up at the end of the evening to compare notes.

11 steps to organising a successful cell social

1. Pray and ask for God's guidance.

2. Discuss: What do you want your next cell social to achieve?

3. Discuss: Who do you want to invite?

4. Decide what to do so you can achieve what you want to achieve and make sure it is suitable for those you want to invite.

5. Choose someone to be responsible to organise it and then delegate the jobs which need to be done.

6. Discuss any potential problems. For example; if you're organising a meal, is anyone vegetarian?; if you're watching a film, what would be appropriate and what wouldn't be? Are there any people who are likely to be coming who might not get on and what are you going to do about it?

7. Pray about any potential problems and for those whom you want to invite.

8. Get on with inviting your friends and getting it organised.

9. Meet together before the event to discuss what you want to achieve, any last minute things that need to be sorted and to pray.

10. Enjoy the social and have fun!

11. At some point after the event talk about what happened, evaluate it and pray.

Training and courses

It has been said: 'So far as evangelism is concerned, those inside the church and those outside it are in complete agreement: they both hate it' (Nick Pollard). Over the years there has been a lot of bad evangelism, and the word evangelism still freaks most people out. Evangelism is not easy and we all have a lot to learn but it should be a natural part of our Christian life.

It would definitely be a good idea to do some cells on evangelism. There are some cell outlines in *Synergy* which look at the topic of evangelism directly or indirectly, for example:

- Back to Basics, Cell 10 (page 68)
- Blueprint for Life, Cell 2 (page 80)

There are many different training packages that will teach you more about relational evangelism. I would recommend that you speak to your cell supervisor and/or cell network co-ordinator about running one for your cell members.

Praying for friends

If you don't pray for your 'witness' you are not going to get very far. There are hundreds of ways you can do this. It is important to pray for events that

THE WITNESS SECTION

are happening, the world as a whole, your country, your town, your community and your school or workplace. However, as well as praying for the general, it is very important that we pray for the specific and see God answer our specific prayers. In this section we will look at praying for our friends; in the next section we will look at praying for wider groups of people.

A good way to pray for your friends is to get every member in the group to choose two or three non-Christians friends they want to see become Christians. When you meet together update each other on any progress that has been made with these friends. Set targets of what you want to achieve, then tell the rest of the group. You are more likely to do it as you wouldn't want to be the only person at the next meeting who hasn't done what they said they were going to do!!

Below are a few ideas on how you can pray in and out of cell. Remember these are only basic ideas, take them, use them and develop them.

- Make a large paper cross, get everyone to write the names of their non-Christian friends on it. You could also write a few prayer points about these people next to their names. Then each week you could use this cross, get people to share anything that has happened in the last week and what they want to happen in the next week. Then as a group pray for the names on the cross.

- Have variety in your praying: sometimes pray as a whole group, sometimes pray in pairs, sometimes go round the group and get everyone to pray for the person on their left, sometimes pray in silence, sometimes pray with music and sometimes all pray out loud together.

- Always remember to share answers to prayer to encourage one another.

- Don't just pray for your non-Christian friends but also pray for each other as you try to bring them in contact with the gospel. Pray for opportunities, courage, strength, encouragement, boldness, protection and the gifts of the Holy Spirit. You could split your cell group into smaller groups (twos or threes). These small groups could serve a number of purposes, including accountability groups, prayer partners/triplets and support outside cell. These groups could pray more specifically for each other and their non-Christians friends in and out of cell. Encourage them to meet up between cell meetings to discuss what has happened and pray together.

- Have regular prayer times, for example, before or after school, to pray specifically for friends or other current issues.

- Have a prayer chain. This is so you can easily pass prayer requests around the group. Have one person at the top of the chain, and if anyone has a prayer request they contact this person. Then they contact the next person on the chain, then that person contacts the next person on the chain and so on.

- It is very important that we do pray for each other and each other's non-Christian friends outside the cell meeting. Create some form of sheet with people's names on it so they can pin it up somewhere as a reminder. You could produce a 'prayer wall'. Write the names of all your cell group in a central wall, then above or below each member write down the names of their two/three non-Christian friends. The idea is that you want all the 'loose bricks' (your non-Christian friends) to become part of 'the wall' (your cell group).

- Be creative: you might what to be artistic in remembering the names of people you are praying for. You could make a huge banner or perhaps actually build a wall out of shoe boxes. On each shoe box you could write the name of one person. Have a slot in each shoe box, then each week you could write down what you want to achieve with that person and put it in the box.

Praying for wider groups

Here are just a few ideas of other things you could pray for during your witness section and how you could do it. Whenever you pray for issues try to find out as much information about them as possible so you can pray specifically, but also remember to let the Holy Spirit lead your prayers.

- Choose a mission agency/missionary and make it your 'focus' agency/person for prayer. Find out information about them/it and get on their mailing list. Pray for them regularly in and out of cell.

- In much the same way you could choose a country and find out about it and pray for it regularly.

- Pray for your village/town/city.

- Over several weeks gather newspaper articles (either local or national) of situations you could pray for. For example, issues or people in power.

- Pray for the group that your cell is attached to (eg. church or cell network) and pray that as a whole you would be effective in your outreach.

- Pray for specific events and outreach projects that are going on in your area.

- Go on a prayer walk in the area where your cell meets. (For example, school, workplace, housing estate, community.)

- Make a big world map and lay it on the floor. Have a few prayer points for each continent then pray creatively for the world.

Practical projects

Christians are called to be salt and light to this world (Matthew 5:13-16), we are called to make this world a better place. It's so easy for us to be so concerned about telling people the gospel we don't bother to do anything about other areas of their life. There is no point telling a starving person about the love of Christ if we don't first show them the love of Christ by giving them something to eat. If we look at Jesus he was concerned with every aspect of a person's life – social, physical and spiritual. If as Christians we're called to be like Jesus, we also should be doing this.

In this section there are just a few ideas of how we can get stuck into practical projects as a cell group and make a difference in our community.

- Help an organisation like the Salvation Army work with the homeless for an evening a week.

- Take it in turns helping as a volunteer at a hospice, children's home, homeless shelter, hospital, etc. (Your cell could commit to providing two people every Monday night, for example, then within your cell you could have a rota.)

- Litter picking (in your school grounds or around where you live).

- Helping the elderly with their shopping, household tasks or gardening.

- Write to your local MP about issues that concern you.

Run a sponsored event. This could have many purposes, to raise money for a good cause, to raise awareness about an issue, to show that your cell group wants to serve the community and to help your cell group gel together.

There are 101 projects you could raise money for; here are just a few ideas:

- for a special event
- for your church
- for a missionary agency
- someone in your cell undertaking a gap year
- for a local charity (for example, those working with the disabled or homeless)
- aim to buy a piece of equipment for your local hospital
- if your cell group meets in your school you could raise money and give it to the school to spend on a specific project.

Whatever you raise money for, try to make it as specific as possible. There are many reasons for this, one being that people are happier to give to something specific and secondly, it will give you as a group something clear to aim for.

There are many things you can get sponsored for, here are just a few ideas:

- car wash

- long distance run
- 24-hour famine
- 24-hour silence
- sleep out (sleep outside in cardboard boxes for the night)
- play a game for 12 hours non-stop (e.g. football, pool or table tennis)
- practical work (e.g. paint a hall at your church or clean your church's windows)
- abseil.

Try to get as much publicity about what you are doing as possible. It's good for people to see that Christians are doing things to make the world a better place.

- Perhaps you could even get onto local TV/radio or into the local newspaper.
- Find out if there are any locally run projects (such as anti-rasicm, unemployment awareness) and see if you can get involved.
- Collect recyclable items, these in turn can often be exchanged for money which you could put to a good cause.

The Witness section with non-Christians

What do you do in the Witness section if there are non-Christians in your cell group? This is a difficult question. If you have a non-Christian in your cell only occasionally then the answer is fairly simple, use some of the suggestions in the 'Praying for wider groups' section. However, what do you do if you have non-Christians in your cell every week? You can't very well pray that your non-Christian friend will become a Christian while they're sitting next to you.

First of all you must realise that it is great that you have non-Christians in your cell, it's a huge positive, not a negative. Just by the fact you have non-Christians in your cell means that you are probably doing the Witness section well. Remember also that the cell structure is meant to help you not hinder you; it's a guideline not a rule. So first point – don't worry!

It is important that you adapt each cell meeting to the people who are there, so always be open to hear from God and let the meeting be led by the Holy Spirit. There are many things you could do in the witness section when you have non-Christians there every week. Here are some suggestions:

- Use one of the ideas from the 'Praying for wider groups' section.
- Organise to do a practical project.
- Use the time to try and answer any of their questions about Christianity.

- Use the time as a general prayer time, encouraging the non-Christians to share things they want to see happen.

It is, though, important that as a cell you continue to pray for the non-Christians and for each other as you seek to share the gospel with your friends. You don't have to do this at a cell meeting. Cell is all about lifestyle, not just one meeting a week. So pray for each other outside the meeting, phone each other, meet in smaller groups at other times throughout the week to discuss how you are doing with your non-Christian friends.

Introducing non-Christians into cell

The step between a cell social and a normal cell meeting is a very big one and is very scary for both the Christian and their friends. How do you make your cell group suitable for non-Christians to come along to see what it's like? It is here where the whole discipleship vs. evangelism pull comes in.

Each cell is unique, each non-Christian who comes to a cell group is unique and different. There is no text book method, it's going to be different for everyone. You need to pray about it; you need to try and work out what is suitable for the non-Christians and the Christians; you need to strike a balance; you need to have faith; you need to be prepared to try new things. You'll learn by trial and error. You need to accept that you will make mistakes, but not to worry about them. God is bigger than your mistakes: learn from them and move on. But remember, don't be ashamed of your faith and be honest. Non-Christians will respect you for that; they need to see Christianity as it is. Too many Christians have tried to put a fake mask on Christianity that does not work, so let's be real with ourselves and our friends.

Below are a number of options you might like to consider; think about them, pray about them, mix and match them and come up with your own strategy for your cell group.

- Carry on as normal. Run the cell as you normally would, try to involve any non-Christians as much as possible and make them feel comfortable. Make them feel that it is OK just to observe what is going on if that's what they feel comfortable doing. You might like to adapt the worship and the word sections slightly so they feel able to join in. For example, for the worship section you could ask everyone to share something really good that has happened to them in the last week and then get a few people to pray thanking God for these things. Also during the prayer time make sure you ask them if they have anything they'd like you to pray for.

- Look at relevant issues. Many non-Christians want to know the Christian perspective on issues. There are many moral issues which people have many differing opinions on. Why don't you occasionally in cell discuss one of these issues? You don't have to make the discussion overtly

Christian, however, throughout the discussion you could explain how being a Christian affects your view on a subject. Possible issues could include, abortion, sex, the environment, designer babies, creation vs. evolution, technology and the supernatural.

- Run a 'Christian basics course'. There are many courses that are available to introduce people to the Christian faith. These are very useful for both Christians and non-Christians alike as they help Christians understand more about their faith and take them back to basics. They are also good for non-Christians as they begin to explain what Christianity is all about. Running a course like this in your cell is an excellent way to blend both discipleship and evangelism as both Christians and non-Christians alike will learn. Many of these courses are very easy to adapt and fit in to the cell structure. Courses available include 'Sound Foundation' (available from Viz a Viz), 'Get God' (from the World Wide Message Tribe) and the 'Alpha' course.

BACK TO BASICS

Introduction

This series of ten cells is designed for new cell groups. Back to Basics looks at what cell groups are, why we have them and what the 'cell values' are. It also looks at some of the basics of the Christian life such as prayer, worship and listening to God.

This material is designed to be very user-friendly as I realise that, as it is being used for new cell groups, you might be a new leader! It is important that you familiarise yourself with the material and Bible passages well in advance of the cell group meeting and that you talk through any concerns you have with your cell supervisor. You will probably need to adapt the material and make it relevant for your group.

Leading a new cell group can be challenging and hard work, but it can also be very rewarding. One difficulty can be that attendance is very varied as lots of different people give cell a go. Doing a series can therefore be quite difficult. However, in this series the first few cells are fairly similar so it should be possible to recap bits and fill people in on what they have missed.

Finally, here is some advice on leading a new cell group from Angela Freed (a cell leader at Northgate High School in Ipswich).

'As a cell leader, starting out with a new group can be hard. You need to draw people out, draw people closer to each other and help them draw closer to God. Remember to pray for the members of your group regularly and ask for God's help in doing this.

'One problem you might have is when you ask a question and get faced with a deadly silence as no one dares speak. Here are a few pointers on how to overcome this:

- Go round the group, directly asking each person.

- Firstly share your view then ask three others.

- Get them into pairs to discuss the questions then let them feed back to the rest of the group.

- You could even give an extreme opinion to provoke a response. Then ask someone whether they agree or not.

Key tips

- Facilitate, don't dominate.

- Keep Jesus at the centre.

- Be direct and to the point.'

SYNERGY

Cell 1: The model of cell – the early Church

Welcome

As this is likely to be your first cell, the Welcome section is very important. Don't worry if you spend a long time on it. One of the first things you need to do is find out people's names. Here are some possible icebreakers you could use. Choose one of them or think of your own:

- Get everybody in the group to share their most embarrassing moment.

- Line up some chairs (one chair for every person in the group), then all stand on the chairs. With or without talking get everybody to get into height, age or alphabetical order – without falling off the chairs!

- Find out three things about a partner (the weirder the better!), then tell the rest of the group about your partner.

Worship

Get everyone in the group to think of an object or give each person in the group an object, (e.g. Tippex, scissors, alarm clock, chocolate or tea bags). Once everyone has thought of/been given an object, get them to think how that object relates to God. (For example, Tippex could talk about God's forgiveness, getting rid of the mistakes.) You could then lead this into a time of prayer, thanking God for the different parts of his character that the objects represent.

Word

Introduction

In this word section we will be looking at the early Church and how it relates to your cell group. It is really an introduction to what's to come. This cell is to get people thinking about what they want the group to be like. Many of the passages used will be revisited in more detail in future cells.

If you look at the early Church shown in the Bible, you will see that it is very similar to what a cell group should be like. For example, they frequently met in small groups, they were a strong community and they also met in big meetings. This is exactly what cell groups should be like – meeting in small groups and also going to big meetings, the two complementing each other. There are obviously things you can do in a small group that you can't do in a big meeting. However, there are also things you can do in a big meeting that you can't do in a small group. You might want to look at this as part of this cell.

Cell outline

For this cell it will probably be useful to have some big sheets of paper and some marker pens, so you can write down the answers to some of the questions.

Ask the people in your group the following questions:

- When you hear the word 'Church' what do you think?
- What don't you like about Church?
- What do you like about Church?

Split up into pairs and get each pair to look at one of these passages. Ask them to think about what Church should be like according to that passage.

| Acts 2:42-47 | Romans 12:4-5 | Ephesians 4:11-17 |
| Ephesians 2:19-22 | 1 Peter 2:5 | Hebrews 10:24-25 |

Get each pair to feed back what Church should be like according to the Bible.

Following on from this, get people to discuss what your cell group should be like. They will probably come up with ideas that are very similar to the values of cell. Along with their ideas share with them the purpose of cell and the cell values.

The purpose of cell

- Love God
- Love one another
- Love the world

The cell values

1. Jesus at the centre
2. Everyone grows
3. Everyone has a role
4. Living the life together
5. Multiply by reaching out
6. Belong before you believe before you behave

Witness

Make a large cross out of paper on the floor. Get each person in the group to write the names of two or three non-Christians friends on it. Then pray for all the names written on the cross. Don't throw the paper away at the end of the meeting – you'll need it again next week!!

If there are non-Christians in your group you'll have to be sensitive about what you do in the Witness section. If you are stuck, speak to your supervisor about it.

SYNERGY

Cell 2: Community

Welcome

Here are a few ideas for icebreakers you could use:
- Bible character charades. Split the group into two teams, then get one person from one team to act out a character (which they pick out of a hat) in front of their team. If their team guesses it correctly, they get two points. If they don't within one minute, let the other team have one guess at who it is. If they get it right they get one point.
- Play Twister™ (available from all good toy shops).
- What are the three main things you look for in a friend?

Worship

Rewrite a Psalm in modern-day language. Psalm 23 is a good one to do.

Word

Introduction

It is hard to suggest what you should do in this section as it will depend on what you covered last week.

Last week was mainly spent looking at what Church should be like. Community is clearly a very important part in this. Therefore, many of the passages you looked at last week were about community. It is quite possible that you have already talked about a lot of the issues. In this cell you really need to make those verses and issues apply to your specific cell group.

By the end of this cell meeting it would be good if, as a group, you knew where you were heading: How do you intend to become a Christian community? What is expected of each cell member to make this happen?

Cell outline

Read Hebrews 10:25.
- Why is it important for us to meet together?

Read the following passages and then discuss some of the questions below. Remember to keep your cell group in mind. What does it mean for *your* group?
Acts 2:42-47
Romans 12:10, 14-21
1 John 3:17-18, 23-24

- What is a community?
- As a cell group you should be a community. Why? And what does it mean?
- What's the difference between your cell community and another community, for example a chess club or dance group?

On a large piece of paper brainstorm the following:
- The things that would damage your cell community.
- The things that would help your cell community.
- The characteristics of your cell community? (The things that should be coming up are discipleship, servanthood, prayer, vulnerability, commitment and care.)

To finish, discuss how important it is that everyone makes an effort to create, keep and own this community. Pray together and ask God to help you as individuals and as a group to achieve what you have discussed.

Witness

Using the same piece of paper you wrote on last week, get the people in your cell group to share briefly about the friends whose names they wrote on the cross. Then get each person to set a target for what they want to achieve with each friend over the coming week or so. For example, try to arrange to go out with them, invite them to a cell social or try to have a conversation about God with them. Then split up into twos or threes and pray for each other, asking for God's help to do this.

Cell 3: We've all got something to give

Welcome

Here are a few ideas for icebreakers you could use:

- Play Pictionary™. Divide the group into two, give each group a pen, a large sheet of paper and an envelope with things they have to draw in it. (Make sure both envelopes have the same contents!) One player from each group picks a piece of paper out of the envelope and draws what is written, without talking, miming or using symbols or words. When the group have guessed what's been drawn, someone else picks a piece of paper out of the envelope. Both groups are doing this simultaneously. Set a time limit.
- If you were a chocolate bar what would you be and why?
- Or you could use the beginning of the worship idea as an icebreaker.

Worship

Get everyone to share the coolest thing God has done in their life over the past week or so. Then say prayers thanking God for everything he has done.

Word

Introduction

This week we will be looking at the cell value 'everyone has a role'. As a leader this is something you definitely want to see in your cell, as it means a. you don't have to do so much, and b. you will learn things too.

Everyone has talents and gifts. As part of the body of Christ we each have something to give. If we don't give it, the rest of the group suffers.

Look at it this way: everyone has something to give on a subject. Let's call it a 'block'. In a normal 'big meeting' setting, the speaker will share their one block with everyone present. So everyone goes home with two blocks (the one they already had and the one the speaker gave them). However, if there are eight people in your cell group, each person brings their block. If everyone shares their blocks you'll each go home with eight blocks instead of one. Also, a block on its own isn't that useful but with many blocks you can construct something of use. Some people might not think they have a block to share. However, they might have some sand, someone else might have some cement and someone else might have some water. When you put all these ideas together you get a block!!

Cell outline

Brainstorm on a piece of paper as many gifts/talents/skills/other things you can think of that people could bring to your cell group. (For example, hospitality, a car to give people lifts, being able to put things simply so people can understand it, being able to lead people in worship and being able to make people feel welcome.)

Read 1 Corinthians 12:12-31. Then discuss, with this overall question in mind – What does this passage mean for your cell group?

- What happens to the leg if the eye stops working? (For example.)
- Why didn't God make everyone good at everything?
- What should you do if your cell group is missing something you think is important?
- What happens in your cell group if everyone plays their part?
- What happens in your cell group if people don't play their part?
- Why might people not be playing their part?
- Why is it important for everyone to be involved at a cell group meeting?

Here are a few more passages you might want to use at some point during your cell:
Ephesians 2:10
Ephesians 4:11-16
1 Corinthians 14:26

It might be appropriate to discuss with each other (maybe in smaller groups) what you think each other has to bring to the group. This should be a time of building one another up and encouraging each other! It would also be good to pray for each other that everyone would find their role and be able to play it in your cell community.

Witness

Photocopy a map of your school/community and write on it prayer points for the various areas. Then pray for the different areas of your school. Get the map photocopied so everyone in the cell has a copy and can use it in their personal prayer times.

Cell 4: We're called to grow

Welcome

You can either use this idea, think up your own icebreaker or use an idea from a previous cell that you haven't used!

- Get everyone to draw a timeline in the middle of a sheet of paper, from the time they were born to the present day. Get them to write in the main/most important events of their life. Write the good things on the top half of the paper and the bad things on the bottom half. After everyone has done this, go round and get everyone to talk through their timeline with the rest of the group.

Worship

On a large piece of paper brainstorm as many words or ideas as possible that describe God. Get each person to choose the word that means the most to them at the moment. Then go round the group saying prayers of thanks to God.

Word

Introduction

The Christian life is a journey. Throughout our lives we should endeavour to become more like Christ. Cell should play an important part in this. It should be a safe place for people to grow spiritually. It should be a place where people feel comfortable to discover and practise their gifts, learn about themselves and develop their knowledge and relationship with God.

This cell should challenge everyone in your group to want to grow and to help each other in the process.

We will begin this cell group where we left off last week. In the first passage you will see how everything we've looked at so far is all linked together.

Cell outline

Read Ephesians 4:11-16.

Discuss this passage looking particularly at the fact that we're all called to grow. Also make it clear how all the previous cells link into this passage. It is important that you've read this passage through and have things clear in your own mind before you lead this cell.

Read Hebrews 12:1-3.

The whole Christian life is a journey. We need to grow and become more like Christ. In your group discuss why it is important to get rid of the things that hinder us.

As a cell you want to help each other grow as Christians. Using the following passages, brainstorm on a piece of paper ways you can do this. Remember, a very important part of cell life is accountability.
2 Timothy 3:16-17
1 Thessalonians 5:11
1 Thessalonians 5:14

Pray with each other that you would be able to do the things you've talked about.

Witness

Using the paper cross from your first cell meeting, go round the group and see where people are at with each of their friends. Check whether they've managed to achieve what they wanted to. Then share with each other what you want to happen next. Go round the group praying for the person sitting on your left.

Cell 5: Worship - it's a lifestyle

Welcome

You could either make up your own icebreaker, use one from a previous week or use one of these:

- Get everyone to put in the middle of the group an object/item that best describes their life right now.

- Get everyone to share the best thing that has happened to them this week.

- Pass an object around the group (e.g. magazine or CD); get each person, in turn, to invent an alternative use for the object. Once the ideas have dried up use another object.

Word

Introduction

In our churches today there is great variety in the way we worship God. Although there is often much tension between the different forms, this shouldn't be the case. We need to affirm the different styles of worship. As we are all different we all prefer to worship God in a certain way. For example, some people find they worship God best with song. Some people can't stand singing but can dance, so choose to express their worship to God by dancing.

This cell could go in many different directions. It really depends on the people you have in your cell.

If you all go to the same church it will probably be very different than if you all go to different churches.

Although worshipping God is an important part of our meetings, what biblical worship is really about is lifestyle; everything we do should be worship to God.

Cell outline

On a large piece of paper brainstorm some, or all, of the following questions:
- What is worship?
- Why do we worship things/God?
- How can we worship God?
- What do you find difficult about worship?

Read each of the following passages and discuss what they mean for you as an individual and as a cell group.

Romans 12:1
John 4:23, 24
Ephesians 5:15-20

Discuss how you want to use the Worship section of your cell group.

During the session encourage people to share their personal experiences of worship, both good and bad. It might be appropriate to pray about the bad experiences and the things people find hard about worship.

Worship

Try to get hold of a copy of Matt Redman's 'When the music fades' (*The Heart of Worship*). Play this and get people to sort things out with God regarding worship.

Witness

Discuss ideas for a cell social and organise it. Pray for the people you want to invite along.

SYNERGY

Cell 6: Prayer

Welcome

Here are some ideas if you need them!
- Who, from all of the past, present or future would you most like to have a one-to-one with?
- How long was your longest ever phone call? Who was it with, what was it about and who paid the bill?

Worship

Use the Lord's Prayer to worship God. Be creative!

Word

Introduction

Prayer is one of the greatest privileges we have as Christians. It is a direct line to God – both ways! What's even more amazing is that the God of the whole universe listens to OUR prayers and acts upon them. We worship a God who answers our prayers.

However, many Christians really struggle with prayer. Whether it's finding the time, knowing what to pray or having doubts whether or not God really answers.

This cell, as with any other cell, depends on who's in your group and where they are at on the whole subject of prayer. The cell is written on three different levels. Choose which level you need to start at and which level you need to focus on.

It is really important that you learn from each other. Encourage people to share how they struggle with prayer. The chances are that someone else in the group will have had similar struggles in the past but found something that helped them.

Our prayers change the world. So in this cell group, by learning how to pray more effectively, you could change your own community and the world!

Cell outline

Level 1

Ask and discuss all, or some, of the following questions.
- Do you pray?
- What is prayer?

- Why do you pray?
- What do you pray about?

Then read James 5:13-18 and discuss what it says about prayer.

Level 2

Discuss what prayers should include. You might want to look at the Lord's Prayer and/or another model of prayer. One model of prayer you could look at is the ACTS of prayer:
- Adoration – worshipping God for who he is.
- Confession – asking God to forgive your sins.
- Thanks – thanking God for what he's done.
- Supplication/shopping list – asking God to act, intercession. (Intercession is to pray 'on someone else's behalf'. So it can include praying for friends, relatives and situations in the world.)

This model of prayer does not include listening to God. We will spend a whole session looking at listening to God next week.

Level 3

These are two very common problems people have with prayer. Spend some time discussing them.

1. 'I find it hard to find the time and keep my mind focused.'

In your cell group discuss with each other exactly what you find difficult. Also, share ideas on how you can solve the problem. Go away and try these ideas out – holding each other accountable.

2. 'What's the point? – God seems to answer so few of my prayers.'

Have a look and discuss what the Bible has to say:

1 John 5:14, 15   James 1:6   James 4:3

Encourage each other by sharing answers to prayer.

This area causes problems and raises questions for many people. If you're not too sure on the issue yourself speak to your cell supervisor about it before the cell. It might be good to get your cell supervisor to come to this cell group and help you.

At the end of this section it would be good to have a massive prayer session. You could use the ACTS model of prayer, and/or read Philippians 4:6-7 to start your prayer time.

Witness

Pray for people in your community and especially your non-Christian friends. Remember to pray as if you are praying to the Creator of the whole universe, who hears and answers your prayers.

Remember, God often calls us to be the answer to our own prayers.

Cell 7: Listening to God

Welcome

Think up your own icebreaker or use one of the following:
- Ask: Who have you spent the most time with in the last week? How much time did you spend with them?
- Ask one person to choose a movement (e.g. winking or crossing their legs). The person next to them has to do that movement and one of their own; the next person does the first movement, the second movement and then one of their own and so on.

Worship

Read 1 Peter 2:22-25. Get everyone to spend a few minutes in silence thinking about these verses and thanking God, but also listening to hear what God has to say. After this go around the group getting people to say prayers of thanks to God.

Word

Introduction

Last week we looked at prayer; hopefully, at some point, you would have touched on the fact that prayer is a two-way process.

It is said that we have two ears and only one mouth; therefore, we should spend twice as much time listening as we do talking. I believe that this is also true of prayer. We need to stop just telling God stuff, and listen to him.

Listening to God is very difficult. We live in a busy, proactive world where sitting around listening to God might often seem like not doing anything. However, it is important that we do spend time listening to God. If we spent more time listening to God, asking him what he wants us to do, we wouldn't waste so much time doing the things we thought were a good idea, but which God didn't.

This cell needs to be led with care as you don't want it going off track, especially when you spend some time listening to God at the end of your group. In the past, too many people have said things and said it was from God even when it wasn't. There are many precautions you can take, the most effective one is this: God never says anything that goes against the Bible.

Cell outline

Read Amos 3:7 and Psalm 25:14. Discuss how amazing it is that God chooses to communicate with us.

On a large piece of paper, brainstorm all the ways God communicates with us (see list below).

Here is a list of some of the different ways God communicated with people in the Bible. You might want to refer to some of them during the cell.

- Angels (Luke 1:26-38)
- Dreams (Genesis 37:1-11)
- Writing on the wall (Daniel 5:5, 6)
- Direct conversation (Exodus 33:11)
- Audible voice of God (Matthew 3:17)
- Via people (1 Samuel 3)
- Prophecy (1 Corinthians 12:10)
- His word (Psalm 119:9-16)
- Visions and pictures (Isaiah 6:1-8)
- Inner voice (Isaiah 30:21)
- Tongues and interpretations (1 Corinthians 12:10)
- Holy Spirit (1 Corinthians 2:10)
- Words of knowledge (1 Corinthians 12:8)
- Symbols e.g. the rainbow (Genesis 9:12-16)
- Signs and wonders, e.g. burning bush (Genesis 3), wind/earthquake/fire (1 Kings 19:11-13).

Then, as a group, discuss which methods God normally uses to communicate with them. Emphasise that the most common way God chooses to communicate with us is through the Bible. So if we want to hear God, we need to read the Bible. Talk about the things people find difficult about listening to God and see if anyone else in the group has already overcome that difficulty.

Spend some time as a cell listening to what God has to say to you or to someone else/the whole group through you. Remember to expect God to speak (but if he doesn't, don't worry and think you've failed, remember God's timing is best). Either do this in complete silence or with some music in the background. After you have done this, share with each other (if appropriate) what God has said. Then pray together about what God has said. This part needs to be led with great sensitivity. Remember these two things: God is love, and God never says anything that goes against his word, the Bible. It might be best if you get your supervisor to come in and help you lead this.

Witness

Once again go back to the paper cross and share with each other what is going on with your friends at the moment. Set new aims and then split up into pairs to pray that God would help you do these things. Remember to be specific when you pray.

Cell 8: Lifestyle

Welcome

Use one of these ideas or think up your own.

- What type of car best describes your Christian life at the moment? What car would you like your Christian life to be like?
- Play Taboo™ (available from all good toy shops).

Worship

Either use CDs, or, if you have someone musical in your group, get them to use their instrument(s). Use songs to worship God.

Word

Introduction

Being a Christian is a full-time job! It's not just something we do in church on Sundays. We have been called to live in the world but not be of the world (John 15:19). This is no easy task and something we can only do with God's help.

This cell looks at some of the areas where we need to be different. An important part of cell is that you help each other live the right lifestyle.

As a cell you can pray, support and encourage each other. When one member falls down, the others can help them up. Also hold each other accountable that you are living the lives you want to live as Christians. (If you're not exactly sure what 'accountability' is, make sure you find out from your cell supervisor.)

Cell outline

Read 1 Timothy 4:12.
Then discuss each of the keywords. Below are some ideas of the sorts of thing you could discuss for each 'keyword'.

Speech

- How should a Christian's speech be different from that of a non-Christian?
- What does the Bible have to say about swearing and dirty jokes? (Ephesians 4:4, 12 and Titus 2:8)

Life (some versions say *conduct* instead of *life*)

- Does the way you live your life make it obvious that you're a Christian?
- Why do we need to practise what we preach?

Love

- Why does God want us to love everyone?
- What does that mean in practice?
- How can we set an example in love?

Faith

- What is faith?
- How can we set an example in faith?

Purity

- What does it mean to be pure?
- What stops us from being pure?
- What areas do you struggle with? (Probably best to discuss in single-sex groups.)

Either as a whole group, in single-sex groups or in pairs, discuss specifically what you struggle with. Then pray for each other.

Witness

Split up into twos or threes and prayer-walk around your area. You could use the map you wrote prayer points on to get ideas about what to pray. Before you split up and go round the area, pray that God would show you what to pray for. If possible, it would be good to meet up afterwards and feed back what you prayed about and anything God told you while you were prayer-walking.

Cell 9: Loving the lost

Welcome

Here are a few ideas of icebreakers you could use:
- Ask the question: If your house burnt down tonight, which three things would you take with you?
- Have you ever lost anything? What was it? How did you feel?
- Play hide 'n' seek.

Worship

God loves us!! Read Zephaniah 3:17; John 3:16 and 1 John 3:1. Then, on a sheet of paper, brainstorm how you feel knowing God loves you. Then praise God either by singing a song or by praying.

Word

Introduction

We live in a world that is lost and has gone away from God. However, God still loves those who are lost and he is longing to see them found.

But, do we love the lost? Do we really understand what it means to be lost and what happens to the lost?

It's having a heart for the lost that should motivate us to do evangelism. In this cell we will look at two things: how God feels about the lost; how we should be sharing what we have with the lost.

In next week's cell we will be looking at some ways in which we can reach the lost, even if they don't realise they are lost.

Cell outline

Read Luke 15:11-31.

Discuss the following questions:
1. How do you think the father felt
a) when his son decided to leave?
b) while he was away?
c) when he saw him coming back?
d) during the welcome-home party?
2. How does this relate to how God feels about people in the world today?

Read Luke 15:5-7.
There is a party in heaven when someone becomes a Christian.

Read Genesis 12:2-3.
This was God's covenant with Abraham. It basically says 'Blessed to be a blessing'. As Christians, God has blessed us with a relationship with him and eternal life, so we should be blessing other people by telling them about him and what he has done for us.

In your group brainstorm all the ways in which God has blessed you (as individuals and as a group), and as Christians in the western world, how we can bless others.

Witness

Pray that God would show you how he feels about your non-Christian friends. Pray that you would begin to understand how God feels about the world and what he wants you to do about it.

Cell 10: Go for it! - Do evangelism

Welcome

You can either use this idea, think up your own icebreaker or use an idea from a previous cell that you haven't used.

- Get everybody to share the thing they are most scared of.

Word

Introduction

This cell is very different from the other cells in this series. It is more of a 'training session' in friendship evangelism. You might actually like to get someone else in to lead it – perhaps your cell supervisor or someone else who is passionate about evangelism. If that isn't possible, you can use the ideas below.

This cell will give you an opportunity to practise evangelistic techniques on each other. You can find out what works and doesn't work in a safe environment where it doesn't matter if you make mistakes.

Encourage everyone to have a go and get stuck in.

You are welcome to photocopy pages 69 and 70, if you feel it would help if everyone had a copy.

Go for it!!

Cell outline

We have already looked at how important it is that we live a Christian life and practise what we preach. However, many people have fallen into a trap summed up by this quote from Bill Hybels (*Becoming a Contagious Christian*, 1994):

> *Far too many Christians have been anaesthetised into thinking that if they simply live out their faith in an open and consistent fashion, the people around them will see it, want it, and somehow figure out how to get it for themselves.*

Discuss this quote. Is this how you are? Why are people so scared of doing evangelism?

Read John 3:16-17 and discuss with each other what the gospel is and how you can communicate it with your friends.

A good way to talk about the gospel and Christianity with a non-Christian is by sharing your story with them (although the gospel might not always be in your story). Unless they accuse you of lying they can't really argue with it. Get everyone to spend five minutes preparing their story, then split up into twos and practise presenting them. It would be good if one of the leaders had already prepared their story so they could share it with the whole group as an example. On the next page there are some pointers as to how to go about preparing 'your story'.

Preparing your story

- So your story has an order to it, split it up into three sections:
  BC – Before Christ – what your life was like before you became a Christian.
  ☨ – Conversion – how you became a Christian.
  AD – After Christ – how your life is different now you are a Christian.

- Don't try to cram in too much information, keep it simple. It is often a good idea to have a central theme. For example, God as friend, God's forgiveness or God's power.

- Don't use spiritual jargon.

- As you share 'your story' make sure the other person is following and understanding it.

- Finish off by asking a question. For example, 'Can you relate to any of this?'

After everyone has shared their story, get the other person to feed back on what they thought about it. You could use the criteria below.

	Bad				Good
Was it too long or too short?	1	2	3	4	5
Was there any spiritual jargon in it?	1	2	3	4	5
Was it clear?	1	2	3	4	5
Did they make sure you were following?	1	2	3	4	5
Was it communicated in a way that made you think that this person was really pleased they were a Christian?	1	2	3	4	5

Split the group into pairs, then get them to do one or both of the role plays on the following page. After this, feedback as a whole group how they found it. Ask some people to share how they answered the difficult questions.

Role plays

Number 1

Location	A coffee shop
Person A	Themselves
Person B	An atheist who really does not like Christians. Starts the conversation by asking one of the following questions (and isn't satisfied with any of the answers given to them by person A):

- Isn't it narrow-minded for Christians to think that they're right and everyone else is wrong?
- How do you know that God exists?
- If a loving and powerful God really exists, why doesn't he do something about all of the evil in the world?
- What about innocent people who suffer, like little children? Why doesn't God do something to help them?

Number 2

Location	A coffee shop
Person A	Themselves
Person B	You are very near to becoming a Christian. However, you have one major problem with the whole Christian lifestyle – there are too many rules. The two main problems about becoming a Christian are these: you'd be expected to stop getting drunk and stop having sex with your 15-year-old boy/girlfriend. Basically, becoming a Christian would really spoil your fun.

Witness

Read 2 Timothy 1:7-9.

Then pray that God would enable you to tell the good news to your friends in a relevant way. Pray that your cell will grow as you see your friends become Christians. Believe that these things are going to happen!

BLUEPRINT FOR LIFE

Introduction

The Sermon on the Mount is a very hard-hitting preach, which very few preachers today would dare to deliver. It shows us just how radically different we're meant to be. It sets the standard for us and proves how much we need God to make it as Christians.

I hope that through studying the Sermon on the Mount you and your cell will be challenged to live the life Jesus has called us to live. The Sermon on the Mount has been described over the years in so many ways. However you describe it, and however you interpret it, it is our 'Blueprint for Life' as Christians.

This passage is challenging and at times you will wonder if you ever will make it as a Christian. The question I asked many times when I first studied the sermon was, 'Does the Sermon on the Mount actually point towards us being saved by good works? But surely that would go against the gospel message.' It's a question that needs answering, and one I think needs answering right at the beginning.

Over the years convincing claims have been put forward supporting both sides of the argument. But I firmly believe that the Word of God doesn't contradict itself and the Sermon on the Mount supports the gospel message that we are saved by grace and not good works. The first beatitude (Matthew 5:3) brings this home, when it makes it clear that we have nothing to offer.

John Stott in his book[1] looks at it like this: The Sermon on the Mount is a kind of 'new law' and it has two divine purposes. The first is to show non-Christians that they can't please God by themselves and therefore directs them to Christ to be saved. Secondly, it shows the Christian who has been saved through Christ how they should live to please God.

Luther puts it like this, 'Christ is saying nothing in this Sermon about how we become Christians, but only about the works and fruit that no one can do unless he already is a Christian and in a state of grace.'

As a leader you will have to do a lot of preparation for each cell you lead, far more than with any of the other material in *Synergy*. Each section has some background reading and then some outline ideas of how you can use it in your cell meeting. There is so much that can be written about the Sermon on the Mount that it was extremely hard to condense it into a few paragraphs. What is written in the background reading is far from the complete picture. I have read many books while preparing this material and I would encourage you to do the same. I have recommended a number of books of various depths at the end of the material.

Whatever you do, you need to take the material given to you here, plus any other information you have and put a cell together that is appropriate for those in your cell group. Most of this material is written with a Christian 'audience' in mind. However, much of it could be easily adapted if there are non-Christians in your cell. Never put a cell together without much prayer and guidance from God.

Cell 1: The Beatitudes (Matthew 5:1-12)

Background

These introductory verses to the Sermon on the Mount are all about the Christian's character. The Beatitudes, as they are called, are not a mix 'n' match selection. We can't choose to have some and ignore others, we need to be yearning for all of them.

As Christians we are part of the kingdom of God: we are primarily residents of God's kingdom, not earth. These verses show us what the characteristics of someone living in this kingdom should be. How do you match up? If you showed one of your friends this list of characteristics, would they say that you matched up to it?

After a quick look at the word 'blessed', we will briefly look at each of the eight Beatitudes and what they mean.

The search for happiness . . .

Most people want to be happy. We spend much of our lives looking for things that make us happy. Many people write Christianity off as a way to introduce happiness into their lives. They would say that Christianity is boring. As Christians we need to be addressing this – perhaps there are far too many people in our churches who aren't happy. However, Christianity isn't about being sad and boring. Jesus said that he came to give us life and life to the full (John 10:10b). You might be wondering what on earth this has to do with the Beatitudes – well, let me explain . . .

The word 'blessed' comes from the Greek word 'makarios' which can also mean 'happy'. So instead of reading, 'Blessed are those . . .' it could read 'Happy are those . . .'. Now blessed and happy both have slightly different meanings and I think that by using the word happy we do lose something. However, we must not lose the happy part from the word blessed. Happy has become a very superficial word. To be happy does not mean to go around with a smile on your face all the time. Happiness is about being content, joyful, at peace with the world and much more. To be blessed is to be happy. So as Christians let's be happy, and let us show the world that we're happy and why we are so happy.

The blessings

Each of the Beatitudes comes with a blessing. The question that is often asked is, 'Are these blessings now or in the future?' I suppose this is one of the many questions we will never be sure about until we get to heaven. However, I am pretty sure that the answer is actually both. The blessings are for both the present and the future. The first and the eighth Beatitude are written in the present tense, but the others are all written in the future. Throughout Jesus' teaching he talks about how we enter and become part of the kingdom of God now. When we enter the kingdom, we can be comforted now, we can receive mercy now, we can become children of God now. So, we receive many of these blessings in part now, and to a greater degree in the future.

Blessed are the poor in spirit...

To be poor in spirit is to realise that we have nothing to offer; we don't deserve anything other than to be judged by God. This first Beatitude is proof that the Sermon on the Mount doesn't go against the gospel. It recognises that we need God, to know God – we can't get to God on our own. The only way we can get to God is because of what Jesus did on the cross. We need to recognise that before we can come to God. We need to realise that, however many good deeds we do, we still won't be good enough.

In Isaiah 66:2b it says 'This is the one I esteem: he who is humble and contrite in spirit . . .' Throughout the whole Bible it is clear that the kingdom of heaven is not a kingdom for the rich, strong, proud and self-reliant, but a kingdom for the poor, weak and humble, who come before God and say 'without you I'm nothing, I need you . . .'

Blessed are those who mourn...

In a sense, this Beatitude seems to contradict itself. To mourn is to be unhappy, but blessed comes from the same word as happy, so it's basically saying 'Happy are those who are unhappy . . .' So what's going on here? The second Beatitude follows on from the first. Once we realise that we are spiritually poor we should be mourning the fact.

We should also be mourning over sin. We should be mourning over the sin in our own lives and over the sin in the world. Now that is a challenge for us as Christians. We are surrounded with sin all our lives: it's around us at school, at work, on television – we just can't escape it. Unfortunately, how many of us have just learnt to accept it? How many of us mourn over the sin in the world?

However, those who mourn will be comforted. In the present we can be comforted by knowing that Jesus died on the cross to forgive and take away our sin. We can also look forward to the future when there will be a new heaven and a new earth and sin will be no more.

Blessed are the meek...

The first Beatitude was how we assess ourselves, especially before God. The second beatitude is to do with our reaction to this. The third is more about our relationship with others than with God.

The dictionary definition of meek is: 1. humble and submissive, suffering injury, etc. tamely; 2. piously gentle nature.

Now meekness is a quality that the world sees as a weak one; it goes against the grain, but as Christians we are called to be meek. However, we must not view meekness as the world does: we're not called to be weak, feeble and trodden underfoot. Jesus was meek and he certainly wasn't weak, feeble or trodden underfoot, was he?

So what does it mean to be meek? Dr Lloyd-Jones[2] sums it up like this:

> *Meekness is essentially a true view of oneself, expressing itself in attitude and conduct with respect to others . . . The man who is truly meek is the one who is truly amazed that God and man can think of him as well as they do and treat him as they do.*

Blessed are those who hunger and thirst for righteousness...

Over the years you have probably heard the word righteousness a lot, but what does it mean? In the Bible there seem to be three areas of righteousness: legal, moral and social. Legal righteousness is all about our relationship with God. Are we right with God? Has God set us free from our sin of the past? Moral righteousness is all about our character and conduct, which so much of the Sermon on the Mount is about. Does it please God? And finally, social righteousness is about society as a whole. Are we promoting civil rights, integrity, liberation from oppression and justice?

What do you hunger and thirst for the most? Is it a better computer, car, the latest CD by your favourite band, more friends or more wacky experiences? Whatever you hunger and thirst for, I doubt that for many people it will be righteousness. However, it is clearly written here that we are to hunger and thirst for righteousness. We must not chase after material things, we're meant to chase after spiritual things. We are to 'seek first the Kingdom of God' (Matthew 6:33).

If we are chasing after spiritual things, it is often lots of other things, but rarely righteousness. Some chase from conference to conference to get some special blessing, some chase from worship event to worship event to get that special buzz – you get the idea. Now going to conferences and worship events and getting blessed by God is definitely not wrong. We should hunger and thirst to get close with God, and conferences and worship events can help us do that. However, we must remember that this isn't what it's all about. We must remember that we should hunger and thirst for righteousness.

Blessed are the merciful...

There is often much confusion between mercy and grace. Richard Lenski[3] sums up the difference like this:

> *The noun eleos (mercy) . . . always deals with what we see of pain, misery and distress, the results of sin; and charis (grace) always deals with the sin*

and guilt itself. The one extends relief, the other pardon; the one cures, heals, helps, the other cleanses and reinstates.

Another definition that has been used over the years is this: 'Mercy is not getting what we do deserve. Grace is getting what we don't deserve.'

This Beatitude is telling us that we should be merciful to those around us. Are we? Do we really show mercy to those around us? Do we help those in need? Or are we so wrapped up in our own lives that we carry on without noticing the problems of others?

God has shown us the greatest mercy and grace, so surely our response to that should be to show mercy and grace to others?

Some have used this verse, along with Matthew 6:14, to say that it is only if we show mercy to people that God will show us mercy. Using this approach is very dangerous and goes against what mercy and grace actually are.

Blessed are the pure in heart...

When Jesus spoke these words 2000 years ago, the people around him were very familiar with the Pharisees who tried to keep hundreds of laws outwardly to gain acceptance from God. Throughout the Sermon on the Mount Jesus challenges the outward keeping of rules, and says, yes, we should do this but it's the inside attitude that is more important.

Christians today have a bad name for being hypocrites, for saying one thing and doing another. How often as Christians do we act in a certain way just because we think we should, while on the inside we are thinking something totally different. What do you do when that dirty joke is told at school or at work? Do you a. laugh with everyone else, knowing on the inside that it's not right; b. don't laugh with everybody else because you're a Christian, but on the inside you wish you could laugh as you actually find it quite funny; c. you laugh with everyone else and haven't got a problem with it at all; or finally d. you don't laugh outwardly, and you don't laugh inwardly, in fact you're disgusted by it? I guess for most of us it's options a, b or c, but as Christians we need to get to option d. We need to be single minded, our actions need to match up with what we are thinking on the inside, and what we're thinking on the inside needs to match up with God's will. It's not just our actions that need to please God, but our thoughts, our whole being.

Blessed are the peacemakers...

It is not good enough just to live peaceful lives or to want peace, we need to get out there and be peacemakers. We live in a very troubled world so there is much we can be doing.

Jesus was the best peacemaker who ever lived. By dying on the cross he made it possible for there to be peace and reconciliation between God and man. We need to continue Jesus' work in bringing peace between man and God by sharing the gospel. However, I don't think we should stop there (although this is the greatest kind of peacemaking we can do). We would be contradicting ourselves if we didn't try to bring about peace in all areas of life.

The world is full of broken relationships and Christians should be setting a different example. How many Christians have grudges and broken relationships with other Christians? What sort of witness is this to non-Christians? How many Christians have broken relationships with non-Christians, which need sorting? And how many Christians are sitting waiting for the non-Christian to take the first step to reconciliation? What on earth are we doing? As Christians we should know the importance of reconciliation and the cost that has to be paid to achieve it. After all, we are only reconciled with God because Jesus died on the cross. So how can we sit back and leave broken relationships broken? We need to be getting out there and reconciling the relationships we are involved in.

It shouldn't even stop there. I think that as Christians, leading by example, we should be the catalysts who help people reconcile broken relationships with others too.

Blessed are those who are persecuted because of righteousness...

Persecution is certainly not a pleasant experience, however, we should be blessed by it as it is a sign that we are doing things right. If we're being persecuted because of our faith it means that the people who are doing the persecuting know about our faith, which is a positive thing to start with. The fact that they're persecuting us probably means that we have hit a raw nerve somewhere and we're making them feel a little uncomfortable about themselves, which also can be a very positive thing.

Persecution can take many forms. Whether it is being rejected by your friends or family for becoming a Christian, laughed at by your work colleagues because you won't take a longer lunch hour or lie on your time sheets or whether it is having verbal abuse hurled at you when you deliver your church magazine to the houses in your neighbourhood. No persecution is pleasant. However, next time you experience persecution, be encouraged and stick it out. God is with you and is pleased that your relationship with him is so high on your priority list that you are prepared to suffer persecution.

Character challenge...

So are you ready for the challenge? Are you ready to shape your character as God wants it, are you ready to stand out as being a resident of the kingdom of God?

Cell outline

Introduction

You could spend many weeks looking at the Beatitudes in your cell group – perhaps you will want to do that.

I have written this cell in two sections. The first section looks at the Christian character described in the Beatitudes in general. The second section looks at each of the Beatitudes in turn.

It is up to you to choose how you want to tackle them in your cell group. You might just want to work your way through one of the two sections, or you might want to combine both. You might want to do this as a very quiet, reflective exercise, or you might just want to go through each of the Beatitudes and get people to think about their own lives in silence. You could use some of the questions in section two to do this. There are many, many ways you could use this material in your cell group. Pray and ask God what he wants you to do.

In the first cell you do on the Sermon on the Mount you might like to give a brief introduction to the Sermon and what you will be doing for the next few weeks.

Section 1: The Beatitudes – the character of a Christian

Read Matthew 5:5-12 and discuss the following questions:

- What does it mean to be blessed? (Bring in the fact that it can also be translated 'happy'.)

- From the Beatitudes, what are the characteristics of a Christian?

- Which of these do you think you already have and which do you think you need to work on? (You could assess each other's strengths and weaknesses if you feel comfortable doing this.)

- Do you think that having characteristics like these would make you happy and help you live life to the full?

If there are any Beatitudes that people don't understand, spend some more time on these. Perhaps you could refer back to the background reading or look at some of the questions in Section 2.

Get people to spend some time alone with God, reading through the Beatitudes again, asking God to show them which ones they need to work on and how they need to do that. Then split up into smaller groups and share with each other about what you have gained from looking at the Beatitudes. Then spend some time praying for each other.

Section 2: The Beatitudes - a closer look

Blessed are the poor in spirit . . .
- What does it mean to be 'poor in spirit'?
- Why do we need to be in this position of realising that we are 'poor in spirit'?
- What do you find the hardest about coming humbly before God and admitting you need him?
- Do you feel you are where you should be at the moment? (Perhaps you could get everyone to spend some time in silence considering where they are at the moment.)

Blessed are those who mourn . . .
- What should we be mourning over?
- What in the world upsets you the most?
- Get everyone to spend some time looking at their own life and if there is any sin in their life that should upset them. Get them to lay it before God.
- How do you think we are/will be comforted?

Blessed are the meek . . .
- How does the world view meekness?
- What does it really mean to be meek?
- Discuss what Dr Lloyd-Jones[2] said about meekness:

Meekness is essentially a true view of oneself, expressing itself in attitude and conduct with respect to others . . . The man who is truly meek is the one who is truly amazed that God and man can think of him as well as they do and treat him as they do.

Blessed are those who hunger and thirst for righteousness . . .
- What things in this world do you most hunger and thirst for?
- What things do you make an effort to get and what do you do to get them?
- Would you say you hunger and thirst more for spiritual things or material things?
- What spiritual things do you hunger and thirst for?
- What does it mean to hunger and thirst for righteousness?

Blessed are the merciful . . .
- What does it mean to be merciful?
- What is the difference between grace and mercy?
- How can we show mercy for others?
- Spend some time thanking God for his mercy and grace.

Blessed are the pure in heart . . .
- What does it mean to be pure in heart?
- Get people to think individually about the things they struggle with inside that no one outwardly knows. If you think it is appropriate you could divide into smaller groups to discuss and pray about these things.
- Get everyone to write down on a piece of paper something that is preventing them being 'pure in heart', and throw it into a bin in the middle of the room and lay it before God.

Blessed are the peacemakers . . .
- What does it mean to be peacemakers and how can we do it?
- Are there any relationships you are involved in that need reconciling?
- How can we help others restore their broken relationships with others and God?

Blessed are those who are persecuted . . .
- Have you ever been persecuted? How?
- How did you deal with it?
- How did you feel while it was happening and looking back on it now?
- It might be that as a cell you are being persecuted at the moment. Pray about it and be encouraged.

You could pray individually or as a group about the things that come up and things you want to change about your character either as you go through, or at the end.

SYNERGY

Cell 2: Salt and light (Matthew 5:13-16)

Background

These verses tell us how as Christians we are meant to live in the world. To do this, Jesus selected two metaphors. The two things he chose were salt and light. In Bible times these were essential items every home would have had, however poor they were. Jesus communicated in a way relevant to his culture. Are we relevant when we communicate Christianity in our culture?

We are called to be the salt of the earth, but what does that actually mean. Let's take a look at the qualities of salt.

Salt...

. . . has a healing, cleansing influence. Salt on an open wound stings, but it does clean the wound and therefore helps the healing process. We live in a hurting world. As Christians we can help bring healing by leading people to Jesus. However, like salt, it stings. As Christians we have to tell people things they don't necessarily want to hear; that we have all sinned, that we can't make it on our own, that we have to surrender our own lives.

. . . is a preservative. Before the time of freezers, meat and fish would be covered with salt to prevent them from going bad. Salt stopped the corruption of the meat. In the same way, Christians should be trying to stop the corruption going on in society. We don't seem to be too good at this. Some become so detached from society they don't really know what's going on around them, whilst others become so involved in society that they themselves become corrupt. Being a Christian in our society is very hard, but then did Jesus ever say it was going to be easy? We are called to live in the world but not be of the world.

. . . enhances flavour. Often people will add salt to their cooking to enhance the flavour of it; food without salt can often taste bland. Well, this might surprise you but Christians are meant to add flavour to the world, making it a more exciting place. If this is the case, why is it that most people think Christians are bland and boring? Well, the answer is simple, we're not being the way Jesus called us to be. Take a look at Jesus for a moment. He had friends, his actions made many enemies, people gave up jobs to follow him, he was respected, he went to parties, he mixed with outcasts, he was radical, he totally smashed people's views on women in society, he made people think, he stood up for what he believed and he was one of those people who seemed to be able to relate to every type of person. That's not what I call bland or boring!! The difficult part is: What are we going to do about it?

These are just three of the many qualities of salt, but we have a lot to learn from these.

Losing saltiness

Salt (sodium chloride) cannot actually lose its saltiness as it is a very stable compound. So, you might ask, why did Jesus use this metaphor? Well, take a look at these two reasons why salt can become useless:

- The first is a bit scientific!! In those days there were no refining processes, so their salt would come straight from the shores of the Dead Sea. These slabs of salt were mixed with a lot of impurities. One of the things they used these slabs of salt for was to put between layers of fish as they transported them to the market. However, when these slabs got wet, it was the sodium chloride that was the most soluble, so it would get washed away. What was left was just white powder that was useless. They would get rid of it by spreading it on waste ground.

- Salt mixed with impurities can become useless and even dangerous. In fact, it is so useless it can't even be used for manure.

That's why as Christians living in this world we need to be so careful. It would be easy for us to get so mixed up in the ways of this world that we no longer stand out as Christians. If this happens we would be like salt that had lost its saltiness.

On many occasions in the Bible Jesus is compared to light. He himself said, 'I am the light of the world,' and in the Sermon on the Mount he tells us that we are to carry on being the light to this world when he is gone. So, as we have done with salt, let's take a look at light.

Light . . .

. . . shows up imperfections. If we're going out to a party with our friends we spend ages getting ready. We first try to make the best of our faults, we then spend ages making sure that not one single hair on our head is out of place. We then make sure our clothes look great. We make sure that everything we are wearing matches and there are no horrible stains on them. However, if we're going to a firework display we rarely spend as long getting ready. Why is that? Well, because at a party it's likely to be light and people can see what we look like. However, at a firework display it is dark so some of what you might think of as imperfections are hidden. As Christians we are meant to be like that. We are meant to live good, pure lives that please God and show up the imperfections of the world. If all the Christians in the world were doing this it would be far more noticeable who was a Christian and who wasn't. Unfortunately it's not often like that. Do our actions really set us apart from the rest of the world? I can remember from when I was younger a quote on a picture that hung in our church lounge; it said, 'If you were arrested for being a Christian, would there be enough evidence to convict you?' Challenging, isn't it?

. . . makes us feel safe. If you are walking home late at night, you would probably try to walk the way that has the most light. If there was a choice between a dark alleyway and a brightly lit road most of us would choose to take the road, even if it was slightly longer. As a child I could never sleep unless the landing light was left on and my door left slightly ajar to let a bit of light into my bedroom. So what? What has this got to do with being a Christian? First of all, people should feel safe around Christians. We should act with integrity and not get ourselves into compromising situations, especially when we are working with children and young people. Also, Christians should be the type of people others turn to if they have a problem. In Ipswich we have cell groups in many of the schools. I believe it to be an excellent sign that the cell group is being a good witness if people turn to the members when they have problems and need someone to talk to. However, when this happens we must again act with integrity and not abuse our position.

. . . leads the way. At sea ships will steer their way between lit buoys and they will use lighthouses as markers and know that they are near shallow water or rocks. Aeroplanes use lights leading up to and on the runway to guide them in their descent. As Christians we should be leading the way. We should be the kind of people that people follow. Also, as Christians, we should be taking a lead in all areas of life, including business and politics. Just think what a difference it would make if the majority of the members of Parliament were Christians seeking God in all the decisions they made.

Shouldn't be hidden

I often find (I know it's true of myself) that Christians try to hide the fact that they are Christians. Whether it's because we're ashamed of our faith or too scared of having to answer questions, it shouldn't be the case. We should stand up and be counted. Street lights stand out, they are put in places where they can be seen – that's the whole point of them. It would be very hard to hide a street lamp. So why do we spend so much of our time hiding away? It's hardly surprising that people reject Christianity and the Church if many Christians are ashamed of it.

Good deeds

Doing good deeds is one of the main ways we are going to stand out and people are going to notice that we are different. However, we're not to do good deeds to make ourselves feel good or to get praise for ourselves. It says quite clearly in verse 16, '. . .that they may see your good deeds and praise your Father in heaven.'

It's evangelism! They say actions speak louder than words; that's often true in evangelism too. People see by our actions that we are different and they then start to question why. This then gives us the opportunity to talk to them about why we act differently from the rest of the world. In doing so we are pointing them to our Father in heaven.

Cell outline

Introduction

In this cell we will be looking at how living as salt and light in the world is a method of evangelism.

In many respects, this passage is a second introduction to the Sermon on the Mount. The first introduction was the Beatitudes – what the character of a Christian should be; the second challenges us to stand out. The rest of the Sermon on the Mount goes on to tell us how we can achieve these things.

You might like to skip this cell and come back to it later and use it more as a conclusion. If we live out the Sermon on the Mount, we will be salt and light to the world.

Read Matthew 5:13-16 and discuss some of the following questions.

Salt...

- What are the characteristics of salt?
- What does that mean for us as Christians?
- What does being the 'salt of the earth' mean in practice?
- What does it mean for us to lose our saltiness?
- How can we lose our saltiness?
- How can we avoid losing our saltiness?

Light...

- What are the characteristics of light?
- How and why do we hide our light?
- What impression does it give if Christians do hide?
- How can we help each other not to hide away?

Good deeds...

- Why is it important that we do good deeds?
- How can we make sure our good deeds point to our Father in heaven?
- What motivates you to do good deeds?

Evangelism...

- Why is being 'Salt and light' an effective form of evangelism?
- Discuss some of these quotes:

   Far too many Christians have been anaesthetised into thinking that if they simply live out their faith in an open and consistent fashion, the people around them will see it, want it, and somehow figure out how to get it for themselves. Bill Hybels[4]

Actions speak louder than words

Preach the gospel at all times, if necessary use words.

Spend some time praying about the matters you have discussed in this cell group meeting.

Cell 3: The Law (Matthew 5:17-20)

Background

It is often easy for us as Christians to keep on sinning. Well, after all, why shouldn't we sin? All our sins have been forgiven. It's by grace we're saved, not by good works, so does it really matter what we do? This passage, along with many more, e.g. Romans 6:1, 2 and 15-18, 1 Peter 2:16, certainly challenges that kind of thinking and should put a stop to it.

On the surface this passage might seem fairly straightforward. However, if you look below the surface, it suddenly becomes a lot more complicated. In writing this material I have read quite a few books on the Sermon on the Mount and spoken to many people. There are so many ways in which these verses can be interpreted and it is very easy to end up tying yourself up in knots. In the next few paragraphs I'll try to begin to make sense of these verses. However, don't take what you read here as fact. I'd encourage you to read and investigate for yourselves exactly what these verses mean. It's often easy to leave the hard passages of Scripture alone, pretending they'll go away if we ignore them!! I'm sorry to break this to you but they won't go away and we really ought to be tackling them head on.

What is the Law?

When we talk about 'the Law' we are referring to the first five books of the Old Testament. The Law was given to the Israelites by God when they escaped from Egypt and became a nation.

Jesus fulfils the Law and the Prophets

There are many ways you could describe Jesus' ministry on earth, but one would definitely be 'he caused quite a stir'. There was certainly a lot of confusion about Jesus' teaching and who he was. Many people were very offended as he seemed to be rubbishing the Law of Moses and turning people against it. His teaching about the Sabbath day certainly gave people this impression. Also, he spoke with such authority and it wasn't just any authority but it seemed to be his own authority – even the evil spirits obeyed him (Mark 1:27). So it was understandable that people were getting a little bit confused about Jesus' authority in relation to Moses' authority. I guess many of Jesus' disciples were beginning to get excited that the days of obeying the Law were nearly at an end. Well, these few sentences sure saw that thought go whizzing out of their heads!!

It is clear from this passage that Jesus came to fulfil the Law not abolish it, but what does this mean? Jesus fulfilled the Law in many ways. John Stott[1] splits it up into three categories:

- *Doctrinal Teaching.* The Old Testament teaches us about God, man and salvation. All the Biblical doctrines (principles) are there, but only in part because it is Jesus who fulfils them and brings them to completion in his person, teaching and work.

- *Predictive Prophecy.* Much of the content of the Old Testament is looking forward to the coming of a messiah (someone to set them free). Jesus fulfilled the prophecies as he was this messiah. The crucial part being his death on the cross in which all the Old Testament ceremonial systems (such as priesthood and sacrifice) found perfect fulfilment.

- *The Moral Law.* The Law of Moses (of which the Ten Commandments forms the base) in the Old Testament is God's moral law for his people. He fulfils this Law in two ways. First, he fulfilled the Law by obeying it. Second, he didn't just obey it, he took it to the next level. We learn so much during the Sermon on the Mount that it's not just obeying the Law outwardly that is important but also what's going on in the inside and our motivations.

Keeping the Law

Jesus makes it quite clear here that we are meant to keep the Law. But hang on. You might be thinking 'What about parts of the Law that talk about the way we deal with mildew in houses (Leviticus 14:33-57), do we really still need to do all that?' Well, there are several points we must note here. In the books of the Law (Genesis to Deuteronomy) there are many different types of law. There are national laws, moral laws, ceremonial laws and laws for the Levites.

So what does that mean for us? We're not from that nation, therefore the national laws don't apply to us, we have to obey our own national laws. The ceremonial laws were all about how they came before God and made sacrifices and so on. Now that Jesus has fulfilled this we no longer need to sacrifice lambs and we don't need a priest to liaise between us and God. Jesus made the ultimate sacrifice and he is our great High Priest and it is through him we can go directly to God. However, it is important that we read and study these laws as it helps us understand exactly what Jesus has done. The Levites were a special group set apart by God. It was from the Levites that the priests came. We are not Levites so the rules especially for them do not apply to us either. The laws we do still have to obey are the moral laws. This means the ten commandments are a good basis.

However, it's important that we don't ignore the parts of the Bible that tell us the other laws. They are still very important. In the same way that it's important to read about the ceremonial laws so we can understand more fully what Jesus has done, it's also important to read the other laws. These give us an insight into the culture at the time the Bible was written. It is crucially important that we always read the Bible in its context. There is also something else we should consider, that is, if God made those laws for the people at that time why did he do that, and is it still a good guide for me as I live my life today?

Righteousness

The next part often confuses people completely. In verse 20 it says that unless our righteousness surpasses that of the Pharisees and the teachers of the Law we won't enter into the kingdom of heaven. Now that seems to contradict much of Jesus' other teaching. Jesus was often getting frustrated at the people who were constantly showing off the fact that they kept the Law so well. Surely it is by grace we enter the kingdom of heaven, not by good works. So what's this all about?

The Pharisees had worked out there were 248 commandments and 365 prohibitions. So does that mean that if the Pharisees had an average score of keeping 235 commandments we, as Christians, need to make sure we keep 240 or we won't get into heaven? No, that's not what it's saying. The problem was that the Pharisees and teachers of the Law made a big thing about keeping all the commandments, the problem was that they were only keeping them at a superficial level. As long as their actions were honourable they thought they were OK. Now Jesus is saying it's not that simple: our motives, our thoughts, what is in our hearts and minds, need to be right too. It is in that way our righteousness should surpasses that of the Pharisees. We also must remember that our righteousness comes through our faith in Jesus.

Fundamental differences

There are some fundamental differences between why we keep the Law and why the Pharisees and teachers of the Law kept the Law. They kept the Law because they thought that this was going to gain them entry into heaven. They were keeping the Law because they thought God would love them more if they did. As Christians we keep the Law not to gain entry into heaven and not to make God love us more. We know that we have been saved by God's grace through what Jesus achieved when he died and rose again. We know that God's love for us is unconditional. We keep his commands because of what he has done for us. It should be our response to the love he has poured out upon us.

Cell outline

Introduction

This is a very complex passage and could easily tie up your cell group in knots for hours! It's probably a good idea not to do that. As ever with this cell material there are many approaches you could take. Below, I've written a possible outline that tries to keep things as straightforward as possible.

However, you might choose to look at the subject at a deeper level and do more of a 'Bible study'. If this is the case you could use some of the information that is given in the background section, plus any other information you come across in your own reading.

Either way, try to keep the focus, keep remembering that it is by grace we are saved. We don't keep the Law so that God will love us – God loves us whatever we do. We should keep the Law as our response to his love.

Remember not to presume that everyone knows what we mean when we talk about 'the Law'. If there are people in your cell who don't know what it means, explain it at the beginning of the cell.

Free to sin?

- Why might we as Christians think we are free to sin if we want to?
- Why shouldn't we have this attitude?
- Use some of the following passages during this discussion:
  Romans 6:1, 2, 15-18
  1 Peter 2:16
  John 8:31, 32
  Joshua 1:8, 9

Jesus and the Law

- Why might people have thought that Jesus had come to abolish the Law?
- What did Jesus mean when he said he had come to fulfil the Law?

The importance of the Law

- Why has God given us so many laws?
- Why should we obey the Law?
- Why is it important to practise what we preach?

Righteousness

- What does it mean to be righteous?
- What does it mean to have righteousness that surpasses that of the Pharisees?

It might be good to finish this section with a time of reflection when people can look at their own lives before God and see if there is anything in it that isn't right. You could then spend some time in prayer either individually or in small groups.

Cell 4: Anger (Matthew 5:21-26)

Background

In Exodus 20 the sixth commandment simply reads 'You shall not murder'. On the surface this seems to be one of the easier commandments to keep. I guess that is exactly what the Pharisees and teachers of the Law thought too. However, Jesus said that our righteousness must surpass that of the Pharisees and teachers of the Law. Here is the first time he begins to expand on this statement. Our righteousness should surpass theirs because their righteousness was a very outward expression; our righteousness must not only be outward but inward. So here, Jesus says, it's not just murderers who will be subject to judgement, those who are angry will also be judged.

The problem of anger

So what is Jesus' problem with anger? After all, didn't Jesus get angry? Take the time when he went to the temple and found men selling animals and exchanging money. He made a whip, turned their tables over and drove them out of the temple (John 2:14-17). Now that sure seems to be anger. It's here we must make a distinction, as there are two types of anger. One we should desire and one we should try as hard as possible to get rid of. The type of anger we should desire is what can be called 'righteous anger' and is the type of anger Jesus shows here. Sin should make us feel angry. Righteous anger can also be referred to as loving anger. It could be compared to a parent shouting at their child to get away from the fire or not to walk out into the road in front of a moving car. This sort of anger is perfectly acceptable. It is how we go about dealing with it where we need to be careful.

The other type of anger is unrighteous, selfish, hateful anger. It is the anger that can burn inside us; it's the hate we feel towards someone else; it is when we even hate someone so much we want them dead. It's no wonder Jesus compares this anger to murder. Being angry towards someone really doesn't do anyone any good. All it does is lead to hate, bitterness and revenge.

Words can harm

The old saying 'sticks and stones can break my bones but words will never hurt me' is untrue. Words can and do hurt and we should watch what comes out of our mouth. If you want to read more about this, read James 3:1-12. But be warned, it's very challenging!

'You fool!' is fairly easy to understand because the phrase is still used today. However, what does 'Raca' mean? Raca is an Aramaic term of contempt and is probably equivalent to the Aramaic word meaning 'empty'. So saying 'Raca' to them would be saying they were 'empty-headed' or an idiot.

The different judgements?

You might have noticed that in the first two verses three different judgements are talked about. The first is simply 'judgement', the second is 'answerable to the Sanhedrin' and the third is 'will be in danger of the fire of hell'. Now this is another part of the Sermon on the Mount people have puzzled over for years. The standard conclusion drawn is this: It seems unlikely that these three judgements are meant to be a progression, in each case getting worse. In the Old Testament God stood behind the whole legal system, so civil judgement was also divine judgement. What Jesus does in these few sentences is move through the accepted route to the ultimate punishment. It is God's judgement that is to be feared the most and it is only God who can make the judgement on what is going on in our heart.

Get it sorted!

The next four verses are all about the importance of sorting things out. So often we tend to let things stay unresolved. At the time this often seems the easiest option. However, it is not the option God wants us to take. Relationships are extremely important to God and so they should be for us.

The first thing Jesus teaches is that if you are offering a gift at the altar and remember you have a problem in a relationship with someone else, go and sort it out before you go any further. How often do we forget to do that today? How often do we try to worship God when our relationships with others are broken? I have been in many worship sessions where I have really struggled to connect with God because my relationship with someone hasn't been right. I try to keep pressing on, hoping that I'll be able to forget the problems and focus on God. However, Jesus says, no, go and sort out the problem, then come back and worship God. I think this same principle is also very important when it comes to taking communion. It's here we are remembering God's ultimate sacrifice and how Jesus died so our sins might be forgiven. How can we do this if we have sins that we haven't repented of?

The next point Jesus makes is concerned with settling matters quickly and not letting them get out of hand. 'It is far better to settle things out of court than in court where the punishment is far greater' (Matthew 5:25). If we do leave matters unsettled they can often get nasty. Wounds fester, bitterness and hatred can eat us up from the inside.

Cell outline

Introduction

Most people probably would not admit to having a problem with anger but for many people anger is a real problem. Often it can lie under the surface and go undetected for years. We can bottle up anger about so many things, but undealt with anger is very dangerous.

In this cell we will look at positive and negative anger, the importance of dealing with it rather than bottling it up and practical ways of dealing with it. This cell might be a time when people can confess things before God and begin to sort out any anger that is stored up inside them.

As a group, brainstorm on a large piece of paper some of the things that make you really angry.

Read Matthew 5:21-26

The two types of anger
(See Background)
- Discuss briefly as a group what the two types of anger are.

Positive anger
- Read John 2:14-17 and discuss the anger shown by Jesus here.
- What things should we be angry about?
- What should we do about this type of anger?
- Are we angry enough about sin, injustice and so on?

Negative anger
- Why is negative anger wrong?
- What harm can it do?
- Is there ever a place for it?
- Is it a good witness for a Christian? Why not?

Dealing with negative anger
- Why is it important that we deal with anger rather than suppress it?
- How should we deal with it?
- Why should we make sure our relationships are reconciled before coming before God?
- Be practical – try not to distance and impersonalise this whole subject. Encourage people to share their experiences. What mistakes have they made? What did they learn from them? What have they found that works, and what have they found that doesn't work?

Be flexible about how you end this section. It might be appropriate to encourage people to share their problems concerning anger and talk in small groups about any relationships that need sorting, and then pray for each other. Or it might be better to put some music on and get everyone to spend some time alone with God, asking God to reveal any anger in their lives that isn't right. Then encourage them to pray through the issues with God.

Cell 5: Adultery, lust and divorce (Matthew 5:27-32)

Background

Sex, love, relationships, lust, marriage and divorce. These topics are all linked and they are all major issues for the Church today. In the past, teaching on these subjects seems to have been avoided, perhaps that's one reason why things are in such a mess. These days the Church is waking up and beginning to realise the importance of good Biblical teaching on these issues.

If you choose to cover these in your cell you should probably seriously consider reading some of the numerous books or perhaps asking someone else to lead the cell who has a better understanding.

Adultery and lust...

Like murder, the Pharisees and teachers of the Law accepted that committing adultery was wrong. However, as with murder, Jesus took it one step further. In connection with murder, he said that even to be angry with someone is wrong; with adultery he goes on to say that even lust is wrong.

Lust is a major problem in our society today. Lust and love are very different. If you want to read about love read 1 Corinthians 13:4-8. Lust, on the other hand, is selfish: it's all about what you want and what you can get. There is nothing wrong with sexual desire if it comes out of love, but lust is a distortion of these desires, it's dangerous and it can get out of control.

The media uses sex to sell things; we are constantly surrounded by sexual images. This is not what God created sex for. He created sex for showing love in marriage, for joining two people together physically, emotionally and spiritually. The media uses sex lustfully. It is wrong and we have to run from it.

Self-control...

In verses 29-30 Jesus describes what we should do if certain parts of our bodies cause us to sin. I don't think we should take these verses literally!! We would all be in severe trouble if we did. I don't think self-mutilation for whatever reason fits with the rest of the Bible as a whole. However, in using this strong language Jesus does get across the seriousness of the situation. We need to control our senses. We need to be self-controlled and we need God to help us do this.

Divorce...

It's hard to know where to start when looking briefly at divorce. Divorce is clearly a problem in our society today. It was also a serious problem in

Jesus' day. Nowadays you can basically get a divorce for any reason, but this goes against the Bible. Jesus makes it clear that the only ground for divorce is marital unfaithfulness (being unfaithful to your marriage partner).

We must realise that it was God who first gave people the option of divorce. It was his loving response to a fallen world. God does not like divorce. He loves the marriage relationship. Love, marriage and sex were all part of his perfect plan.

As Christians it is easier for us to concentrate on the negative; it's easy to go around telling people that divorce isn't an option and that it is wrong. I think that if we do that we have really missed the point and we are coming at it from totally the wrong angle. We need to come from it from the positive angle and that means concentrating on marriage.

The Church needs to be addressing the issue of marriage; it has got to look at why people find it so hard to make it work. It has got to get in touch and provide good quality biblical teaching on the subject. At the moment the Church is playing catch-up, it's trying to repair a lot of damage. The fact is, if there had been teaching earlier much of the damage needn't have happened in the first place.

We need to bring God's plan for marriage back into society's agenda. Marriage and sex is a God-given gift: 'For this reason a man will leave his father and mother and be united to his wife, and the two will become one flesh. So they are no longer two but one. Therefore what God has joined together, let man not separate' (Mark 10:7-9).

Finally, those people who have experienced divorce can often feel rejected by the Church; they feel they have failed and have sinned. As Christians we need to stop the mindset that sexual sins are worse than any other kind of sin. Sin is sin, and sin is forgiven by God.

Cell outline

Introduction

If you choose to tackle these extremely difficult topics in your cell you are going to need to do a lot of preparation. There is certainly not enough information and guidelines in the background reading section of this cell outline.

All I have done below is begin to suggest some of the possible issues you could look at.

Handle this cell with a lot of care, planning and prayer.

Adultery

- What causes people to commit adultery?
- How can you make sure adultery doesn't happen in your marriage?
- Can a marriage survive if adultery has been committed? (If 'no' why? If 'yes' how?)

Lust

You will probably want to tackle this issue in smaller, single sex groups.

- Do you struggle with lust and in what areas?
- Why are we so lustful?
- What can we do about it?

Both adultery and lust need much prayer and accountability to make sure they don't happen. Spend some time praying for each other. If lust is a problem, pray that God would help you deal with it. If there are married people in your cell pray that God would keep their marriages strong.

Marriage and divorce

- What is God's plan for marriage?
- Why is divorce so rampant in our society today?
- What should be the Christian response to this?
- What are the acceptable grounds for a divorce according to Jesus?
- How would you help a friend who's had a divorce/thinking about a divorce/going through a divorce?
- How can Christians make known the importance of marriage?
- What makes a marriage fail?
- What makes a marriage work?

You might like to spend some time praying for some or all of the following:

- Those you know who have been through/are going through a divorce.
- That your own marriages would stay strong.
- That you'd be able to help and support those around you.
- That society would once again realise the importance of marriage and that God's plan for it would be recognised.
- What our part in doing this should be.

Cell 6: Communication (Matthew 5:33-37)

Background

We live in a time where communication has never been easier to do, but perhaps it's never been harder to understand.

Communication is constantly happening around the world, whether it is by television, radio, newspapers, letters, the telephone or the Internet. We can contact practically anyone, anywhere, at any time. What we communicate and how we communicate it is an extremely powerful force. We can build people up or we can destroy people. We can tell the truth or we can deceive and adapt things for our advantage. Through what we communicate we have the power to make or break relationships.

This passage in the Sermon on the Mount is all about oaths. It would be very easy for us to tie ourselves in knots over this passage. Oaths are not something most of us think about much these days. However, the passage is still very relevant.

Let's do things in reverse and look at Jesus' conclusion in verse 37 first, 'Simply let your "Yes" be "Yes", and your "No", "No".' We need to think before we speak. We should say what we mean, we should speak honestly and be full of integrity. Once we've said we're going to do something we should do it; we should be reliable and trustworthy.

It is a challenge, as it goes against the grain. We live in a world where most communication is trying to influence us one way or the other, most of what we hear today has some bias to it. As Christians, though, we need to be ambassadors of the truth.

Oaths in Jesus' day...

People in Jesus' day liked making oaths, they were constantly doing it. They were very serious about the ten commandments and did not want to take the Lord's name in vain. Therefore, they went to great lengths to make sure they did not use the Lord's name in their oaths. Instead they would swear by heaven, earth or even their own head. The whole thing had got pretty ridiculous and basically their oaths didn't mean anything anymore.

No oaths full stop?...

We must remember that in the Old Testament people were told to make oaths. In Deuteronomy 10:20 it says, 'Fear the Lord your God and serve him. Hold fast to him and take your oaths in his name.' God himself makes oaths (Genesis 22:16, 17). So if God is against oaths, why did he himself make one? What we have to understand is this: God never wanted oaths to be necessary. If we always spoke the truth we wouldn't need to swear by something to make people think we meant it. However, we live in a fallen world, and as with divorce, God had to make a concession to our fallenness. So why did God make an oath? The fact is God did not need to make an oath, he would never have lied. He made an oath because of our unbelief. John Stott[1] puts it like this 'The fault which made God condescend to this human level lay not in any untrustworthiness of his but in our unbelief.'

So why did Jesus say we shouldn't make oaths, when in the Old Testament God said we could? The answer lies in what oaths had become: They meant so little it totally degraded the things they were swearing by. Basically this was degrading God (Matthew 5:34-36) and was wrong. Jesus is saying, 'Stop making oaths, they're pointless if you don't ever stick to them. Just be honest with each other, let your "Yes" be "Yes" and your "No" be "No".'

Finally, what about oaths these days? In everyday life we shouldn't have to make oaths or swear by things. We should just let our 'Yes' be 'Yes' and our 'No' be 'No'. However, what happens if we have to give evidence in court? We would be expected to make an oath binding us to tell the truth. Some people, who take this passage very literally, would say that you shouldn't make even this oath. However, taking a passage out of context is dangerous and we have to bear in mind many things. To address this issue we can look at another part of Jesus' teaching. Later on he himself is put under an oath and he responds: 'The high priest said to him, "I charge you under oath by the living God: Tell us if you are the Christ, the son of God." "Yes, it is as you say," Jesus replied' (Matthew 26:63, 64).

Cell outline

Introduction

You could do this cell in a number of ways. You could use the background reading and prepare a Bible study on this passage or you could use the outline below, which looks at Christian communication at a wider level. The choice is yours! Either way, make sure you make it relevant for the people in your cell and that they can relate it to their lives today.

Read Matthew 5:33-37 and discuss the following questions:
- What does it mean to always let your 'yes' be 'yes' and your 'no' be 'no'?
- Why is it important that we do this?
- If we do this, there isn't any need for oaths. Why?
- Why shouldn't we swear by things? (For example, heaven, earth or our own head.)
- How and why as a Christian should our communication be different from the rest of the world?

Split the cell into smaller groups and give each group a number of these verses to read and think about. Then come back as a big group and discuss what these verses say about Christian communication.

- Exodus 20:7
- Exodus 20:16
- Galatians 6:1
- Ephesians 4:29
- Ephesians 5:4, 12
- 1 Timothy 4:12
- Titus 2:8
- Hebrews 3:13
- James 3:2-12
- James 4:11

At the end (again in smaller groups) discuss with each other what you have learnt from this cell and anything you need to change about your communication. Then spend some time praying for each other.

Cell 7: Rights and revenge (Matthew 5:38-42)

Background

This next section of the Sermon on the Mount looks at taking revenge and our rights. This passage can easily be taken out of context and we must be careful when interpreting it.

An eye for an eye...

The complete version of this law can be found in Exodus 21:23-25. *Lex Talionis*, as the Law was called, had been around a long time and the principle has been carried out throughout history. Its basic purpose was to limit retaliation. But now, Jesus seems to come in and totally destroy this reasonable principle. Before we jump to any conclusions we need to understand the context. By Jesus' day money had almost certainly replaced the principle in the court of law, i.e. instead of losing your eye you would have to pay an appropriate sum of money, except perhaps if the issue was 'life for life'. However, people were now employing the principle in personal relationships rather than through the courts; they were using it to justify revenge. It is this that I believe Jesus is prohibiting, not the use of the principle in a court of law. In the Old Testament (Leviticus 19:18) God makes it clear that revenge is not right: 'Do not seek revenge or bear a grudge against one of your people, but love your neighbour as yourself.' Jesus is reaffirming the importance of this Law.

Rights...

During this passage Jesus gives us four examples of different rights that we should surrender.

Right to dignity...
Verse 39b, '... if someone strikes you on the right cheek, turn to him the other also.' In Jesus' time, if you were to strike someone with the back of your hand it was the greatest possible insult. Here Jesus is telling us to accept this and not retaliate – a principle he demonstrated in his own trial and crucifixion.

Right to security...
Verse 40, 'And if someone wants to sue you and take your tunic, let him have your cloak as well.' This verse is a lot more powerful than it first seems if we look at what the cloak stood for in Jesus' time. The cloak wasn't just worn during the day, it was the cloak people used as a blanket during the

night, so with no cloak you might freeze. In fact, the outer cloak was recognised as a right by law (Exodus 22:26, 27). Jesus is saying to us that we need to be prepared to give up the things that give us security; we should find our security in Christ, nothing else.

Right to liberty . . .
Verse 41, 'If someone forces you to go one mile, go with him two miles.' Roman soldiers would command people to carry their luggage for a certain distance. This would obviously be a great inconvenience, but Jesus is telling his followers not to resent this forced labour, but to do it willingly. Today, people are very protective of their own time and certainly don't want other people telling them how to spend it. Here Jesus is saying, be willing to give up time for others, don't resent being asked to do something. If your boss asks you to do a little extra work, do it, and do it cheerfully. What a good witness that would be!

Right to possession . . .
Verse 42, 'Give to the one who asks you, and do not turn from the one who wants to borrow from you.' Jesus is saying that we should hold loosely to possessions. We should have an unselfish attitude regarding property, after all, everything we have is given by God. At the same time we must remember that God has told us to be good stewards of what he has given us.

One question that springs to mind is 'What about beggars, should we give money to every beggar?' We have not got time to look at this issue in too much depth. To begin with, money might not be the most appropriate thing to give them, as we don't know how they are going to spend it, perhaps it would be more sensible to give them some food or drink, or help them in some other way. If you are going to take them anywhere, however, never do it on your own, always make sure there are two of you. It would be easy to get extremely hung up over this whole problem, however. I will close this section with this quote from D. A. Carson[5]: 'The issue is not the wisdom or foolishness of lending money to everyone who comes along, just as beggars are not the issue. The burden of this passage is this: Christ will not tolerate a mercenary, tight-fisted, penny-pinching attitude.'

Doormats? . . .
This whole section seems to be saying that Christians have to be doormats. Is this true? No, is the answer to that question, and the following quote from John Stott[1] explains why. 'Jesus' illustrations and personal example depict not the weakling who offers no resistance. He himself challenged the high priest when questioned by him in court. They depict rather the strong man whose control of himself and love for others are so powerful that he rejects absolutely every conceivable form of retaliation.'

Relationships...

It would be easy to take this whole passage very legalistically. If we did this, we would be missing the point. As we saw earlier in the passage, Jesus was referring to our personal relationships. The point is simple, we need to get our priorities straight. We live in a world where people take their rights very seriously. Many put rights before relationships – look at the world of business for an example. As Christians we are meant to be different: we should put relationships with others before our own rights, we are to be considerate of others and not self-centred.

Witness...

As Christians we should stand out as being different. Just imagine how powerful it would be if we lived out this passage: if someone comes up to us and gives us verbal abuse and we just accept it and don't retaliate; if we were looking forward to a night in front of the television but our friend has had a really bad day so we go out and let them share all their problems with us; if we give some money to a single mother so she can afford to feed her baby for another day, which means that we can't buy that CD we've wanted for so long. As Christians we need to put others first. Before we act, we need to think 'What would Jesus do?'

Cell outline

Introduction

As with so many cells in this series I can see this one either being really hard to get your group talking or a really good cell where everyone talks openly and is really challenged to give up their rights and just trust God.

As a leader it could be a hard cell to lead, but pray about it and ask God to guide you as to how he wants you to run this cell.

Read Matthew 5:38-42 and use some of the following questions along with any of the background reading you think is relevant.

Revenge

- Why should we not take revenge?
- Are there any times when revenge is an appropriate option?
- How literally should we take this passage?
- What do these verses mean in practice today?
- Encourage people to share any previous experiences they've had with 'turning the other cheek'.
- Share and pray with each other if there are any situations any of you face

at the moment where you would really like to take revenge. Discuss and pray about what you should do instead.

Rights

Spend some time looking at each of the rights covered here in turn.

Right to dignity (Matthew 5:39)
- What does 'right to dignity' mean?
- How far should we take this verse?

Right to security (Matthew 5:40)
- What does 'right to security' mean?
- Why as a Christian is it important to give this right up?
- How do we give this right up?

Right to liberty (Matthew 5:41)
- Think of some practical examples of how we can do this today.

Right to possessions (Matthew 5:42)
- How can we do this?
- How do we balance giving this right up and being good stewards of our money?

Doormats?

It might seem that the passage is saying that as Christians we should become doormats, but it is not. You might like to spend some time discussing this and looking at how Jesus was definitely not a doormat.

Relationships

This passage is all about how we should place more importance on our relationship with others than our own rights. As a group spend some time discussing this.

Cell 8: Loving your enemies (Matthew 5:43-48)

Background

Once again the Law had been twisted and once again Jesus sets it straight. The Old Testament Law makes it clear that we should love our neighbour but nowhere does it say that we should hate our enemies. It's something people have added to make life easier and justify their actions towards those they don't like. You might also notice that something else has been dropped. There is no mention of our attitude towards our neighbours. We are meant to love them as we love ourselves (Matthew 19:19). Jesus, as he often does in the Sermon on the Mount, take things to another level; he makes it clear that we are to love everyone, saying it's not just our neighbours we have to love but our enemies too.

Praying for them...

In verse 44 it says, 'Love your enemies and pray for those who persecute you.' Now that is powerful. We're not told to say that we love them and leave it at that. We are meant to be doing something actively for those people we don't like.

How much time do we spend praying for the people who really get up our nose? Do we pray for those who persecute us or do we just pray that they will stop persecuting us? Well, we should be praying for those we do not like. We should be praying that God would help us love them through our words and actions. We can't do it on our own and the only way we will fully be able to obey this command is if God helps us. We should also pray that our enemies will meet God and be saved. We must remember that at one time we were as far away from God as they are, and God wants to touch their lives as much as he touched us.

Why should we?

Loving our neighbours/enemies is a command for us as Christians, so not doing it is wrong. However, I strongly believe that a loving God doesn't command us to do things just for the sake of it, there is a reason for this command. So what is it?

One reason is because God first loved us (John 13:34). This is a recurring theme in the Sermon on the Mount – God treats us very well indeed, far, far better than we deserve – he loves us, has mercy on us and forgives us. So our response to that should be to treat other people in the same way. We must remember that we have hurt God far more than anyone could ever hurt us and yet he still loves us unconditionally. So how can we hate another person whom God created, whom God loves and wants to spend eternity with?

Think about the problems in the world for a moment. Think about how many of them would disappear if everyone followed this command. It is because people are so self-centred that the world is in such a mess. If everyone loved others as much as they loved themselves the world would be a much better place.

As Christians we should be set apart from the rest of the world. Loving our enemies would be a dramatic demonstration of this and would point others to God. If people saw how we loved our enemies they would almost certainly begin to ask questions, and it's then we can talk to them about God. Verses 46 and 47 make it clear that it is not a big deal to love those who love us, everyone does that. So the only thing that will set us apart is if we love the people who can't stand us.

Be perfect...

There have certainly been many challenging verses in the first chapter of the Sermon on the Mount. Although I don't particularly want to single any of them out, verse 48 probably tops them all: 'Be perfect, therefore, as your heavenly Father is perfect.' Now, what does that mean? Surely we can never reach that stage? Well correct, we can't ever reach that stage until we are in heaven, however, that is what we should be aiming for.

It is not the first time in the Bible that God's followers have been challenged to strive to be like him: 'We are to be holy, for the Lord our God is Holy' (Leviticus 19:2). You might be thinking it's pointless aiming for something you know you will never be able to achieve. It is crucially important that we do so. If we use a manmade standard to judge whether we are being good or not we might reach it but we would then forget how much we need God. However, if God is our standard, we will never be able to make it and we will always remember that we need God to get to God. God himself sets the standard of morality we should be striving for.

Cell outline

Introduction

This is a key command of Jesus. However, in practice, it is very, very tough. Then again, no one ever said being a Christian and living a lifestyle different from others was going to be easy, did they?

Loving those around you is a very important part of your cell witness. So during this cell, put the emphasis on how you as individuals and as a cell can love those around you.

Read Matthew 5:43-48 and discuss some of the following questions:

Loving

- Why should we love our enemies?

- What does the word 'love' mean in this context?
- How do you love people you can't stand?
- Think of people you can't stand and think about how you can begin to love them and show them that you love them. Pray with each other that you'd be able to do that.
- Think as a cell how you can love the community around you.
- If we love those who hate us, what do you think it communicates to a. them and b. others?

Praying

- Why should we pray for those who persecute us?
- What should we pray for?
- Are you being persecuted by anyone at the moment?
- Spend some time praying for those who are persecuting you.

Being perfect

- Read verse 48 again.
- What does this verse mean?
- How do we go about doing something about it?
- Spend some time in silence thinking and praying about this verse.

Cell 9: Giving, prayer and fasting (Matthew 6:1-18)

Background

Chapter 6 concentrates much more on our personal lives as Christians. Firstly it looks at the three disciplines of giving, prayer and fasting. These three subjects are all vast, so as ever we really can't do them justice in the next few paragraphs. We will just attempt a brief overview of each.

Verse 1 is an introduction to the whole section. 'Be careful not to do your "acts of righteousness" before men, to be seen by them. If you do, you will have no reward from your Father in heaven.' It is to the point, we mustn't do things to get the praise of others; in whatever we do we should be interested in pleasing God. We must make sure that our motive for doing things isn't to get the praise of men.

Giving

This passage is not really concerned about how much we give. It just states that we should give money to the needy. What this passage is concerned about though is the motivation behind our giving.

So what motivates our giving? Do we only give to seek the praise of others, do we like to let people know how much we give so as to impress them? Or do we give just to make ourselves feel better, putting something in the collection bag on Sundays because we feel guilty if we let the bag pass by? Both these motivations of giving are wrong.

When we give we shouldn't care about what others think. After all we don't want a reward from others, we want to please God. It says in verse 3 that we shouldn't let our left hand know what our right hand is doing. Now, this clearly isn't a literal illustration. What it is saying is that giving is a very private thing and if we keep our giving private we will avoid being inappropriately rewarded.

Everything we have belongs to God, therefore anything we give we're giving back to God. Also think how much God has given us. How can we hold things back from him? The issue of how much we should give is a big one. We need to handle the whole situation through prayer. We need to ask God what he wants us to give our money to and how much we are to give. Perhaps though even this is the wrong way of doing it. After all God gave us everything we have in the first place, so instead of praying 'How much should I give away?', we should be praying 'How much should I keep?' and be prepared to give the rest away.

Prayer

Jesus, in the Sermon on the Mount, doesn't tell us that we should pray, he already presumes that we do. He begins by telling us how not to pray and then goes on to how we should pray. Again Jesus stresses that it is the motivation behind what we do that is important.

The Pharisees were known for the show they made of praying. They would pray long, loud prayers in places where people would notice them. They were more concerned about gaining recognition from others than with pleasing God with their prayers. The motivation behind our prayers must be right, we mustn't be praying out loud, using the right words to impress others; our prayers must be for God only.

Jesus stresses the importance here of praying on your own where no one can see you. He isn't knocking prayer meetings, it is important for us to meet and pray in groups. The most important issue is what's going on between you and God. The challenge for us is, do we pray more when we are on our own or do we only pray when we're with others?

Jesus also tells us not to babble in our prayers. Our prayers should be to the point, there's no need to babble. God knows what we are going to ask for anyway. When we pray we should seek to pray in accordance with God's will. We should therefore ask the Holy Spirit to direct and guide us.

Effective prayer is prayed with the right motivation, in the presence of God not because of the presence of others, and what is prayed for is in line with God's will and led by the Holy Spirit.

The Lord's Prayer

This prayer is without doubt the most often repeated and well known prayer amongst Christians. However, how many times have you said it without thinking about it? This is the grave danger when words are so familiar to us, we say them without thinking about what they actually mean. Perhaps it would be good to go back, look carefully and meditate on the Lord's Prayer for a while and really get to grips with what it is saying.

First of all we must note what it says in verse 9, 'This is how you should pray'. It does not say 'This is what you should pray'. It's not wrong to use the Lord's Prayer during church services and in our own prayer times, it can be extremely helpful. However Jesus prays the Lord's Prayer as an example of how we should pray. It is a model we can use to base our prayers upon.

The Lord's Prayer is split into six parts. The first three parts are to do with God directly: his name, his kingdom and his will. The last three parts are to do with us: that God would provide for us, that he would forgive our sin and that he would lead us out of temptation. It is important for us to remember this in our own prayers; often we can become so focused on us that we forget God.

Notice how in the Lord's Prayer the words 'our' and 'us' are used, not 'my' and 'me.' This is important. We must not pray in isolation. There is nothing wrong with praying for ourselves but we must remember we are part of the body of Christ, we're part of a larger community and we should pray together and for each other.

Fasting

The Pharisees used to fast twice a week and, as with everything else they did, they made a big thing of it and made sure that the people around them knew they were fasting. Here Jesus, says 'no' to this. Fasting is between the faster and God, and you should not make a scene about it in front of others.

Christians in this country today are very keen that we should give and pray, but for many Christians fasting seems to have got lost. I believe this is wrong and once again we should revisit the importance of fasting. We see the importance of fasting right through the Bible – what makes us think we don't need to do it? Read in Matthew 9:14-15 what Jesus has to say about fasting. He said that when he leaves, his disciples will then fast – we are his disciples.

Why fast?

It is important that before we fast we know why we are fasting. I can only touch on this very briefly here so I'd urge you to read about fasting in some books. Fasting can be seen to add power to our prayers but, as Richard Foster points out in his book *Celebration of Discipline*,[6] this can be a very risky reason to fast. He says 'How easy it is to take something like fasting and try to use it to get God to do everything that we want.' He goes on to say, 'Fasting must forever centre on God, it must be God-initiated and God-ordained.'

Forgiveness and fasting

In the Old Testament fasting is often associated with mourning and repentance. Here are two examples:

- Nehemiah got the Israelites 'gathered together, fasting and wearing sackcloth . . . and they confessed their sins . . .' (Nehemiah 9:1, 2).
- Daniel 'turned to the Lord God and pleaded with him in prayer and petition, in fasting . . . prayed and confessed . . .' (Daniel 9:3, 4).

Prayer and fasting

Fasting is equally used when asking for future mercy. Here are two examples:

- Before Esther approached the king (which meant risking her life) she called a fast (Esther 4:16).
- Christ himself fasted before his public ministry (Matthew 4:1, 2).

Self-control

As humans, hunger is one of our basic instincts. Being hungry isn't wrong, it is our body's warning sign telling us we need to eat something. However, this can so easily lead to one of our biggest pitfalls: greed. We also must remember that 'Food does not sustain us: God sustains us' (Colossians 1:17).

D. A. Carson[5] sums it up like this: 'We have no cause to punish our bodies (for they are God's creation), but we must discipline them to obey us. And fasting is one way of increasing self-control.'

Cell outline

Introduction

These are three vast subjects that you could easily spend at least three cells looking at. It will depend totally on where your cell is at as to how you handle each of these subjects. Below are just a few ideas of issues you could look at and discuss. Use them, plus the background reading and any other material you have, to put together a cell or some cells.

The main emphasis of this cell is to get people to look at their personal life before God. Therefore it might be good if during this cell you gave people the chance to spend some time with God alone in silence, thinking and praying through some of the issues raised.

Giving

Read Matthew 6:1-4 and discuss some of the following:

- What motivates you to give?
- What should motivate you to give?
- What reward do you get from men and what reward do you get from God? Which is better?
- Get everyone to spend some time with God in silence, thinking and praying about their giving.

Prayer

(If your cell group is new to the concept of prayer it might be good to use Cell 6 from the 'Back to Basics' series.)
Read Matthew 6:5-8 and discuss some of the following:

- Do you pray more in groups or on your own? Why? Which do you find hard? Which do you find more beneficial?
- Why should we pray if God already knows what we're going to say?
- What motivates you to pray when a. in a group, b. on your own?
- Discuss how you should pray when you pray as a cell group.

The Lord's Prayer

Read Matthew 6:9-15 and then, using the questions below and the background reading, discuss the Lord's Prayer.

- What are the six parts to this prayer?
- What is significant about these parts?
- The Lord's Prayer is a model for us to know how we should pray. Looking at the Lord's Prayer, what should our prayers be like?

Fasting

- What is fasting?
- Why should we do it?
- Talk about people's past experience of fasting?
- Discuss the practicalities of doing a fast. Perhaps you could even arrange to set aside a day to fast as a cell group.

Cell 10: Treasures in heaven (Matthew 6:19-24)

Background

In this passage Jesus is clearly saying that we shouldn't be storing up material treasures on this earth. As Christians earth is only our temporary residence, we should be looking forward to our eternity in heaven. So it makes sense really. What is the point of storing up treasures on earth when we can't take them to heaven?

Misconceptions

Firstly, let us clear up a couple of misconceptions that people can have about this passage. It doesn't mean that having material possessions is wrong, that would go against what is said elsewhere in the Bible. There is nothing wrong with Christians owning their own homes and having belongings, though we do need to keep everything in perspective. Richard Foster in his book *Money, Sex and Power*[7] puts it like this: 'Perhaps we need to stamp everything in our possession with the reminder "Given by God, owned by God, and used for the purposes of God."' Jesus is not saying we can't have material possessions, he is saying we must put them in their proper place and not let them become idols.

The second misconception people can have from this passage is that of saving. Is it wrong to have a saving account? Is it wrong to have a pension? Is it wrong to store up money for a later date? These again aren't wrong. God wants us to be good stewards of our money. Elsewhere in the Bible the ant is commended for storing up food in the summer so it can eat in the winter (Proverbs 6:6-8). We have a responsibility to be wise with what God has given us (1 Timothy 5:8).

Treasures in heaven

So, we are not meant to be storing up treasures on earth but in heaven. What does this mean, how can we store up treasures in heaven? In reading this passage in isolation it would be easy to fall into the trap of presuming that good works on earth gain us a better place in heaven. However, that goes against the Bible's teaching on grace, etc. So what does it mean? First of all, it has a lot to do with what the rest of the Sermon on the Mount is teaching, that is, the character of a Christian. On this earth we should be preparing ourselves for heaven. We can't take our material possessions to heaven, all we can take to heaven is ourselves. As Christians we are called to become more Christ-like. It is not something that happens overnight, it's a process, a long and hard process. Secondly, we can store up treasure in heaven by living obedient Christian lives on earth. What we do on earth has eternal repercussions. For example, we can spend our money on excess material possessions or we can spend our money on trying to advance the kingdom of God. The former will end up on a scrap heap when it becomes out of date or, even if it does stay with us all our life, it isn't going to heaven with us. The second option though will mean there are more people in heaven (treasure) and fewer in hell. How are you going to spend your money and time?

Vision and direction

This metaphor about eyes being the lamp of the body is a little more complicated than the treasure and over the years there have been several different ways of interpreting it. However, they basically point toward the same meaning.

The eyes are very important parts of the body, nearly everything we do relies on us being able to see. Blind people or people who lose their sight have to learn how to do things differently. Our physical sight guides us, it makes sure that we are heading in the right direction. This passage is talking about our spiritual sight – our vision, where we are heading. If our eyes are good and heading in the right direction then the rest of us will follow. If our eyes aren't pointing us in the right direction, then we'll be heading towards darkness.

In the King James Version of the Bible the word 'good' is replaced by the word 'single'. This is because in the original, the word for good means 'singleness of purpose, undivided loyalty'.

Today we can use this passage when we consider what we watch on TV and read in magazines. What we see in the media has a huge influence on what we do and who we are. So as Christians we should be watching what we look at with our eyes. Is what we are watching/reading letting light into our body, or darkness?

Divided loyalties

So often as Christians today we try to keep a foot in both camps. When we're in church we do the church thing and when we're with the world we go along with the world. Now it is not wrong to stay in touch with the world; we're called to live in this world but not be of the world. If we distance ourselves too much how are we going to do any evangelism? However, we must be careful; we must have only one master. If we are being led by two potential masters we can't be truly loyal to either of them. As Christians we are called to be loyal to God. So, there is nothing wrong with using money but we mustn't serve it.

Cell outline

Introduction

We live in a materialistic world. As Christians it is very easy to get caught up in this. However, this passage goes totally against the materialistic attitude of the world and sets a very different challenge for us as Christians.

Pray that this cell will really challenge you and the members of your cell to set yourselves apart from the materialism of the world today.

Treasure

Read Matthew 6:19-21 and discuss the following:

- What does it mean by 'treasures on earth'?
- What does it mean to 'store up treasure in heaven'?
- Verse 21 says, 'For where your treasure is, there your heart is also.' Where is your heart at the moment?

Get everyone to spend some time on their own with God, thinking about where their treasure is at the moment and what they need to do about it. Then split up into smaller groups and pray for each other.

The last cell was about fasting so perhaps you could encourage people to 'fast' for a week, giving up the treasure on earth that gets between them and God (e.g. don't play any computer games for a week). Be sensible about how you go about this as there are things that it is probably best you don't fast from for a week, for example, food.

- Is it right for a Christian to have a pension plan, life insurance or a savings account? Why?

Vision

Read Matthew 6:22-23 and discuss the following:

- What does this illustration mean?
- How can we keep our eyes good?
- What makes our eyes bad?
- Who/what do you follow/influences you the most?

Serving two masters

Read Matthew 6:24 and discuss the following:

- What happens when you serve two masters?
- What/who do you serve at the moment?
- How can we keep money in its right place?

Split up into small groups and pray about the matters you have discussed today and hold each other accountable.

Cell 11: Worry (Matthew 6:25-34)

Background

When this passage is used today the first word is often missed out. You will notice that this passage starts 'Therefore I tell you do not worry', it doesn't just say 'don't worry'. The word 'therefore' indicates to us (or should) that we need to read the verses before it to get the full meaning of why Jesus is saying 'do not worry'. Directly before this passage we learn about not storing up treasure on earth but storing up treasure in heaven. Therefore it makes sense not to worry about things on this earth.

However, as Jesus so often does in the Sermon on the Mount, he takes the statement 'do not worry' to another level. He doesn't just say not to worry about building up material possessions, he says don't even worry about food, drink and clothes – the basic things of life.

Concern or worry?

The first point we need to recognise is that when Jesus says 'do not worry' he is not giving us permission to be reckless or careless. Our bodies are a gift from God and we should take care of them.

It is helpful to look at the differences between concern and worry. There is nothing wrong with concern, in fact it is a very important part of being a Christian. However, it is when this concern becomes worry that there is something wrong. The problem is that it is much easier said than done, as there is a very fine line between concern and worry. Let's take a look at the dictionary definition of these words:

Concern: be relevant or important to; relate to; be about; interest or involve oneself.

Worry: give way to anxiety or unease; allow one's mind to dwell on difficulty or troubles.

Now it is very easy to cross from concern to worry. To worry is to give way to anxiety, so I believe Jesus is saying that our concerns shouldn't turn into worry.

So what does this mean in practice? Well it's very hard, but it is all about having faith in God, which we'll look at in more detail later. It is quite right to be concerned if a young child goes missing. It is our concern that makes us act by going out and looking for them or praying for the situation. However, we should not let this concern turn to worry, we should be able to place the whole situation before God and trust him.

Nature

Most of us today hardly give a thought to nature. We live in manmade environments and we rely on ourselves to make sure we are kept safe, dry and well fed. At the beginning of the twenty-first century it is often a bizarre concept to stop and really take a look at nature. But try it, we can learn a lot. Here Jesus uses nature to explain his point. He uses birds to illustrate God providing food. When he says God feeds them he is not saying that God gives each bird a few seeds from his hand. He is saying that through the whole nature-system of the world he provides them with food and cares for them. In the same way God cares for us. What good would it do the birds if they worried where they would get their next meal from? It wouldn't benefit them in any way at all, so what good does it do us to worry about such things?

In the next illustration Jesus uses lilies. If we take the time to look around us there is such beautiful scenery that humans had nothing to do with creating. God, however, takes care of it all.

What about the starving people of Africa?

It might be easy to read this passage in the developed world, as most of us have food every day. However, what about the thousands of starving people in Africa; what about all the Christians who are dying there? Why isn't God providing for them? To answer this question we must realise that there is enough food in the world to feed everyone. The reason that people are dying of starvation is because people throughout the world are greedy and selfish and aren't spreading the world's resources around. Also, many people in Africa are starving as a consequence of war, not because their land isn't fertile.

What's the point?

Let us look at it this way: what is actually the point of worrying about tomorrow, what do we gain from it? Well, we don't really gain anything positive from it. We might gain some negative stuff like lack of sleep but nothing positive comes out of it. We waste so much time worrying when we should be concentrating on the present, not the future.

Faith

Our worry so often shows our lack of faith in God. We as Christians should put our faith in God in all things; we should learn to rely totally on God. These days this can be so difficult because the world is telling us a different story. The world is telling us that we are in control and we must make sure everything is OK.

Again we must remember that this passage isn't an excuse for us to be bad stewards of what we have. We should not waste what God has given us. Common sense is a gift from God and we should use it!

The future

So how should we look at the future? Is it wrong to make plans? No, it's not. We should ask God to give us visions for the future and seek his will for our lives. However, we shouldn't be worrying about it. We should learn to place the future in his hands knowing that he knows what is best for us.

Cell outline

Introduction

Worry, stress, anxiety are all major diseases in our society today. They are eating away at people and destroying lives. The disease is as much present among Christians as anywhere else.

Here Jesus brings us a clear message – don't worry, there is no point, God is in control.

This cell is relevant for everyone: make the most of it to discuss what worries/concerns you have, how you deal with them and to pray with each other.

- What things worry you and stress you out?
- Why do we worry?
- What good does it do?
- As Christians why should we view 'worry' in a different form than non-Christians?

Read Matthew 6:25-34 and discuss some of the following:

- Why shouldn't we worry?
- Is not worrying about anything a bit reckless? (Look at the difference between worry and concern.)
- What things should we be concerned about?
- What can we learn from nature?
- Read verse 31. Why are there so many starving people throughout the world?
- How do you deal with worry/stress?
- Why/how can we have faith in God?

Discuss what things are worrying you at the moment and pray for each other. (You might also like to discuss with each other how you think people can deal with their specific worries.) As part of this time you might like to meditate on verse 34.

Cell 12: Judging others (Matthew 7:1-6)

Background

One of the things Christians are known for by the world is being judgemental and hypocritical The world hates it and so should we as Christians.

Do not judge...

This passage simply says, 'Do not judge . . .' However, it is not that simple. Are we not to say anything about right and wrong? What about people like Hitler? Elsewhere, Jesus actually encourages us to make 'right judgements' (John 7:24), so is he contradicting himself? Firstly we must look at what it means by the word judge. The Greek word from which 'judge' is translated can mean a number of different things: to discern; to judge; to be judgemental; to condemn. If we look at the context of this passage Jesus is saying we are not to be judgemental. We should not have a judgemental spirit, always trying to find fault with people and putting people down.

Jesus' audience knew a lot about judgemental people. The Pharisees were renowned for it, always putting people down and making themselves look better. However, as we've already learnt from earlier sections of the Sermon on the Mount, they were no better, they were hypocrites.

Hypocrisy

Jesus hated hypocrisy, as this passage makes clear. What right do we have as Christians to judge others when we're in the same or even worse position than them? When we're striving towards holiness, trying to live our lives like Jesus and we feel we're making progress, it is very easy to think we're finally getting there. We can then begin to look down on others and start thinking they're really not making as much progress as we are. However, we must never forget that it is only due to God's grace that we're where we are. We're no better than them. We've all sinned, we all deserve to be punished and we're all saved by God's grace.

Correction

Elsewhere in the New Testament it talks about how we should point out the sin of others (Matthew 18:15 and Galatians 6:1, for example). Is this a possible contradiction? No, it's not. However, we must be careful that when we point out the sins of others we do it to help them grow as Christians and that our attitude is one of loving concern not judgement. We must always remember that we're no better and it is only by God's grace that either of us can be saved.

Jesus says we can point out other's sins (verse 5) but first we must remove the sin from our own lives. Doing it this way we avoid being hypocritical. Pointing out other's sin and being held accountable is very important. However, it doesn't seem to be a top priority in Christian groups today. This is probably because it has been abused so much in the past. Your cell group would be an excellent place where you could do this. However, remember you need to have discernment, wisdom and a loving concern for the spiritual growth of your cell members. You also need to be prepared for correction yourself.

Dogs and pigs?

Verse 6 is a bit confusing to say the least!! Over the years this has been interpreted in many different ways. Here I'll try to explain a little about what it might mean. I will leave you with two possible interpretations.

Jesus was known for never beating about the bush. He said what he meant. Here he is comparing certain humans to dogs and pigs. Now, he is not talking about nice clean dogs, he's talking about the kinds of dog that roam the street scavenging for food. We must also remember that for the Jews the pig was a very unclean animal and they would not go near them.

Jews would never give 'holy or sacred' food to a dog. (Holy or sacred food might be food that had previously been offered as a sacrifice.) And you certainly wouldn't throw your nice expensive pearl into a herd of pigs, would you? This is all very well, but what is Jesus saying here?

- One of the possible interpretations is that there's no point correcting people who are just going to throw it back in your face.

- Another possibility is that it's about trying to tell the gospel to people who just keep on throwing it back in your face. That is, stop showing people this gift (the gospel) if they keep rejecting it. We must handle this interpretation with great care and not use it as an excuse not to tell people the gospel. It's not saying that if we tell someone the gospel once and they laugh we should give up. This is talking about the continued abuse and hard-heartedness of people. Giving up on someone is a very serious step to take and should only be done after much prayer. This is consistent with what Jesus taught elsewhere, for example in Matthew 10:14.

Cell outline

Introduction

During this cell it would be easy to distance it from your lives and look at the whole issue very vaguely. Try not to do this.

Challenge people to look at their attitude towards others and begin to look at how you want to deal with each other's sin, as a cell group.

Read Matthew 7:1-6.

Judging others

- What do you think the word 'judge' means here?
- Why shouldn't we judge others?
- Get everyone to spend some time thinking whether or not they have a judgemental attitude to others. If appropriate, encourage people to share their thoughts.
- How can we deal with our judgemental attitude towards others?

Correcting others

Read Matthew 6:5, 18:15 and Galatians 6:1.

- What do we do about the sin of others?
- Does it concern us?
- Should it concern us?
- What should we be doing about it?
- Spend some time as a group considering whether or not you want to challenge each other on the issue of sin. Discuss how you are going to go about doing this. You might also want to discuss 'high risk' sin areas in your lives so you can think of specific ways to help each other. It might be appropriate to split into small groups to do this. Always remember to pray.

Pigs and dogs

Read Matthew 7:6.

- What do you think Jesus is getting at here?
- How can we know who the 'pigs' and 'dogs' are?
- What should we do if we are faced with a 'pig' or a 'dog'?

Cell 13: Ask, seek, knock (Matthew 7:7-12)

Background

The first six verses of this chapter were all about our relationship with others. The next few verses move on to talk about our relationship with God, our heavenly Father. Then in verse 12 Jesus sums up all his relationship teaching during the Sermon on the Mount and then he goes on to sum up the whole of the Law and the Prophets.

Ask, seek, knock

We have all probably heard these words so many times. These three words and their attached promises mean so much and over the next pages we will only be able to scratch the surface of the depth of their meaning. Perhaps, after reading these pages, you might like to read through verses 7 and 8 again and spend some time meditating on them, seeking God, asking him to reveal to you some of the meaning of these words.

Persistent prayer

Jesus has already talked about how we should pray, during the Sermon on the Mount. In these verses he calls us to be persistent in our praying. It is so easy for us to pray one short prayer about a situation and that's it. We don't see anything happen so we give up. This is not how it should be. We should pray and we should pray persistently and we shouldn't give up. If we believe that we are praying in accordance with God's will, we should keep praying until we see the answer. We should be passionate about what we are praying for and put our whole being into it.

How many of us just pray because we feel we have to and it is the right thing to do? This shouldn't be our attitude to prayer. We should come to prayer recognising we are talking to God, the Creator of the universe. Prayer releases God's awesome power and when we pray we are calling on the power that created the whole universe.

In these verses it suggests that we will get what we ask for. It often seems that this is not true. There are a number of issues we need to bear in mind here. We must always try to pray in accordance with God's will. So, before we pray, we must find out what God's will is for a situation. Secondly, God is a loving father. Just as an earthly father does not give his children something that will harm them, neither will God give us something that will harm us. God knows us best, he made us, therefore he knows what will harm us and what will be good for us. We might not think so, but we just have to trust God on this one.

Seeking God

We should hold our relationship with God as the most precious and important part of our life. Have you ever had a really brilliant Christmas present, something valuable to you, something you've always wanted? If you have, you will know what it is like to treasure something. Our relationship with God is the best gift we could ever be given and it was bought at a great cost – Jesus died on the cross so we could have it. We must treasure it.

If you have a favourite singer, band or football team, you probably 'seek' after them. You want to know more about them, you want to get the latest album and you want to go and see them play or perform. You also probably spend a lot of time with your friends telling them how good your favourite singer, band or football team is. This is how it should be with God. We should be seeking after him, we should want to spend as much time as possible with him, learning all about him and seeking his will and talking to our friends about him.

How much more worthwhile it is to seek after God. When we seek after God it's a two way thing: God's interested in us, even more than we're interested in him. Now that is almost certainly not true about your favourite singer, band or football team – they probably don't even know your name.

Knocking at the door of heaven

We have learnt from the Sermon on the Mount quite plainly that we are never going to be good enough to get to heaven. However hard we try we are never going to make it. We can do good things all our lives but still we will never be good enough. You might be thinking it's worthless then, what is the point of trying anymore? Well, there is a point. If we seek God, if we knock at the door of heaven, if we ask God to forgive our sins, he will open the door, and he will let us in. We must come to him, recognising the fact that we are poor in spirit (Matthew 5:3) and that we can't get into heaven without his help. We can never earn our way into heaven, the only way in is to seek, knock and ask.

God – the perfect parent

In verses 9 to 11, Jesus talks about how earthly fathers would treat their children, then he goes on to say how much better your heavenly Father is.

We live in a broken world and the father heart of God is a hard concept for so many people to grasp, especially if their earthly father has let them down. How do you say, 'Father God,' when your earthly father gets drunk, hits your mum, hits you, never spends any time with you and never says one encouraging word to you? It is something we need to bear in mind when we communicate the gospel to people. There are many, many people both in and out of the Church who find it difficult to relate to God as father because of their relationship with their earthly fathers.

God, however, is the perfect parent: he will always treat us well. He can be the perfect parent that we never had. He can set us free from the past and begin to heal the wounds.

Conclusion

Verse 12 is the conclusion of Jesus' relationship teaching during the Sermon on the Mount. 'Do to others what you would have them do to you . . .'. We must notice that this is written in the positive not the negative. So often we can twist this and say 'Don't do to others the things you don't want them to do to you.' Although this is clearly part of what Jesus is saying, he is saying far more than that. We are meant to be doing good to those around us. We are the salt and light of the earth and we are meant to be showing people God's love.

As Christians it is so easy for us to isolate ourselves from the world; we can spend so much of our time doing the 'church thing' and spending time with God we forget everyone else. Church is important and spending time with God is vital but we must not forget those around us. God doesn't want us to do that. We need to spend time with them, we need to show them God's love. How else are they going to hear the gospel?

Jesus says that this verse sums up the whole Law and the Prophets. We don't always look at the Bible like this but basically the whole Bible is about relationships. Our relationship with God and our relationship with others. Relationships are the key and we must not forget it.

Cell outline

Introduction

As with most of the material in this series it is written with a 'Christian' cell group in mind. However, if there are non-Christians in your group this might be a very good cell to adapt to be very evangelistic.

Read Matthew 7:7-12 and discuss some of the following questions:

Persistent prayer

- Why do you pray? (For example, is it because you feel you have to, because it seems to be the right thing to do or because you believe that God is going to answer your prayers?)
- What does it mean to be persistent in prayer?
- Why should we be persistent in prayer?
- Do you feel that God answers your prayer?

- Why might God not give us what we ask for?
- How do we make sure we are praying in accordance with God's will?

Seeking God

- Who do you most enjoy spending time with?
- What lengths will you go to, to spend time with that person?
- How much effort do you make in spending time with God?
- How do we get to know God more?

'Knocking at the door of heaven'

- How do we get into heaven?
- What does our attitude need to be like when we knock at the door?
- How can we be sure the door has been opened?
- Get people to share their experiences of 'knocking on the door' and God opening it for them. What is it like outside the door and inside the door?

God – the perfect parent

Handle this section with care as, if there are people in your cell who have been deeply hurt by earthly parents, it could be very painful for them.

- Can you think of things that earthly parents do that point to God our heavenly father?
- How does God differ from earthly parents?
- How do we communicate the 'parent heart' of God with those who have been hurt by their earthly parents?

Jesus' summary of his teaching on relationships

Read and discuss Matthew 7:12. Then pray with each other that you will be able to put this into practice.

Cell 14: Go do it!! (Matthew 7:13-29)

Background

These last few verses seem to be the conclusion of the Sermon on the Mount. Jesus makes it clear that there are only two options, we either go God's way or we don't. There is no half way point, we are either for God or against him.

Two options

So we have only two options and in this passage Jesus illustrates them in a number of ways : We can go through the wide gate and follow the wide road or we can go though the narrow gate and stay on the narrow path. We can be good trees bearing good fruit or we can be bad trees bearing bad fruit. We can be wise and have a strong foundation of rock, or we can be foolish and make our foundation on sand. The choice is ours.

The narrow vs. the wide

We can either go through the narrow gate and walk along the narrow path or go through the wide gate and walk along the wide path.

Before we can go through the narrow gate we first have to find it. The narrow gate is much harder to find than the wide gate (John 14:6 and John 10:7). It is harder to go through the narrow gate than to go through the wide gate. We can easily fit through the wide gate and we can take whatever we like through with us. However, this is not true of the narrow gate, we can't take any of our baggage through with us, we have to go through on our own and totally rely on God. We can't take those things that give us security, we can't take our possessions with us, we have to be prepared to leave everything behind and put our trust in Jesus.

The wide road is a road in which we can wander all over the place; we can do what we want, walk where we want, try the things we want and believe what we want. The other road isn't like that, it is narrow, much like a mountain track where we have to be very careful not to lose our way or our footing. We need a good map (the Bible) and a good guide (Jesus) to survive it.

The narrow path can often feel restrictive. On the wide road there is room to try out lots of things and make our own decisions; that is not true on the narrow path: we have to follow Jesus. However, we must remember what Jesus says in John 10:10b, 'I have come that they may have life, and have it to the full . . .' Jesus hasn't come to make our lives dull and boring, through him we can have a full life. Jesus knows what works and what doesn't work, therefore there is no need to try out all these things (for example, drugs). Jesus knows that they harm us so will keep us from them.

Are we prepared to give up the things that keep us secure and walk through the narrow gate without any baggage? Are we prepared to surrender our own lives completely to Jesus and follow him? Or do we want to keep all our baggage with us and walk the wide road, trying to make it through life on our own? Working out what is good or not by ourselves, doing things by trial and error, knowing that what we are trying could harm us severely?

The two trees and their two fruits

In this section Jesus speaks about how we can recognise false prophets by their fruits. However, we can apply these verses to ourselves as well; the question could also be, are we false Christians?

Jesus says that a bad tree only bears bad fruit and a good tree can only produce good fruit. It is by the type of fruit it produces that we can tell whether it's a good or bad tree. This is the same for all of us, not just the false or real prophets.

The Sermon on the Mount is all about our Character and our Conduct. The Beatitudes are very much about our character, the rest is very much about our conduct. However, it is dangerous to separate the two too much. Let us look at the definitions in the dictionary:

- *Character:* the collective qualities or characteristics, esp. mental and moral, that distinguish a person or thing.
- *Conduct:* behaviour (especially in its moral aspect).

Both of these are very much interlinked, but it is our character that shapes our conduct. It is because of who we are that we do what we do. This is the same as Jesus' tree/fruit illustration. If the tree is good it will produce good fruit. If our character is good, our conduct will be good. If our character is bad, our conduct is far more likely to be bad.

A good or bad tree is spotted by its fruit. Our character is shown by our conduct. The world sees our conduct much more clearly than it does our character. As Christians we should help each other build up and strengthen a good character so the world will then see our good conduct. Your cell group should be a place where people can come and nurture 'their tree' so that 'their fruit' will be healthy and good.

Making sure you are a Christian

Verses 21-23 are all about making sure you are a Christian. Just saying 'Lord, Lord' doesn't make you a Christian, in the same way that just saying 'Man. U' doesn't make you a Manchester United fan. You have to act like a Man. U fan. To be Christian we need to do what Christians should do.

However, some people do what they think a Christian should do, but they're still not a Christian (verse 22). Today many people think that just by going to church, putting money in the collection and reading the Bible, they are Christian. The fact is they are not.

As well as the actions, we need the relationship. We need the relationship with God that we receive when we ask for forgiveness through Jesus' death on the cross. This is just the start of the relationship, like any relationship it takes time and needs to be worked at.

Your foundations

Verses 24-27 tell a very well known story. If you went to Sunday school you no doubt heard this story time after time and you probably have sung many songs about it too. When a story becomes so familiar to us we often miss the point that it is trying to make.

This story is all about making sure we have strong foundations. The world is a tough place for a Christian and if we haven't got strong foundations we will not be able to survive. Like the house built on the sand, we will be destroyed.

So what does it mean to have your foundation on a rock? How can we have a strong foundation? There are many ways we can build a strong foundation. First, however, let's look at the foundations of a house. The builder puts the foundation in first; you can't see it but it is very important, without it the house would collapse. The same is true of our foundation as a Christian.

Our foundation is important, it needs to be built early on and it needs to be strong. Our foundation is also the part that people can't really see. However, like a house with a bad foundation it is fairly obvious on the surface whether we have a good foundation or not. If we don't the cracks will begin to show and we could well collapse.

You might be noticing some connection between this illustration and the previous one about a tree and its fruit. Our character is part of our foundation. Before we work on our conduct and what we are doing for God it is very important that we work on our character and who we are.

Our foundation should be based firmly in Jesus and his teaching. Reading the Bible, studying it, meditating on it, praying and listening to God are all ways to build a strong foundation. Foundations provide support for the house. As Christians we need support from those around us. So our cell group could also be part of our foundation.

Conclusion

There is so much in the Sermon on the Mount it is hard to take it all in. You could easily spend your whole lifetime studying it. We also need to spend our whole lives trying to put what it says into practice. Just to study it and think it's a good idea is pretty much a waste of time – we have to go and do what it says. So . . .

. . . Go do it!!

Cell outline

Introduction

This will probably be the last cell you have in this series on the Sermon on the Mount. Use it to draw together any loose ends you still have.

Spend some time discussing what you have all learnt over the last few weeks/months and how you think your life has changed. Also talk about how you want your life to continue to change, what areas you especially want to work at and how you are going to hold each other accountable.

Below are just a few ideas of what you could discuss in this cell from the remaining verses of the Sermon on the Mount. Remember to use the background reading to help you prepare for this cell.

Go do it!!

The narrow vs. the wide

Read Matthew 7:13-14 and discuss the following questions:

- How do we get through the narrow gate? (It might help to use John 14:6 and John 10:7.)
- What are the characteristics of the wide road and the narrow road?
- How do we make sure we stay on the narrow road?
- Why would we want to stay on the narrow road when it is so difficult?

Character and conduct

Brainstorm on a piece of paper some of the characteristics of the Christian's character you have learnt from the Sermon on the Mount. Then do the same for conduct.

Read Matthew 7:15-20

- How as a cell can we help each other keep our 'trees' (our character) healthy?
- How does good character help us to produce good fruit (good conduct)?
- Why is it important that the world sees our good fruit (good conduct)?

Making sure you are a Christian

Read Matthew 7:21-23

- How do people these days fake being a Christian?
- How do we know that we are a Christian or not?
- What are the characteristics of a Christian lifestyle?

Foundations

Read Matthew 7:24-27

- Why is it important that we have strong foundations?

- What makes a strong foundation and how can we make sure we have one?

Conclude this cell by sharing what you have learnt throughout the whole series. Get everyone to write down things that have most challenged them, things that have changed in their lives and things they want to continue to see changed. Then spend some time praying for each other.

Bibliography

1. John Stott — *The Message of the Sermon on the Mount*
Part of 'The Bible speaks today' series
IVP 1984

2. Dr Lloyd-Jones — *Studies in the Sermon on the Mount*
Combined edition
IVP 1977

3. R. C. H Lenski — *The Interpretation of St Matthew's Gospel*
Augsburg 1964

4. Bill Hybels — *Becoming a Contagious Christian*
Willow Creek Resources 1994

5. D. A. Carson — *The Sermon on the Mount*
Part of the 'Biblical Classics Library'
Paternoster Press 1998

6. Richard Foster — *Celebration of Discipline*
Hodder & Stoughton 1989

7. Richard Foster — *Money, Sex and Power*
Hodder & Stoughton 1985

CHARACTER REFERENCE

Introduction

It's been bothering me for a while now how most cell material is based on the New Testament. We seem very rarely to use the Old Testament in the Word section of a cell meeting. However, there is so much we can learn from the Old Testament.

Character Reference is a series of ten cells on five Old Testament characters. It often seems that the characters in the Old Testament are from a different world and are in a totally different league when it comes to a relationship with God. However, this is simply not true. They made mistakes, they went through times of doubting, they felt inadequate and they got angry, but, God used them all. We must remember that it is the same God who used them who can use us today. God doesn't change.

This material was very hard to write and you might find it hard to lead some of these cell groups. However, I think the topics covered are vital, and I think it is important that we look at issues through the eyes of Old Testament characters. Preparation is going to be crucial in this series. You need to make sure you are familiar with the characters long before you lead a cell on them. If people in your cell are unfamiliar with the story, you are going to need to explain it to them. It would be good for you to do some background reading on some of these characters.

We don't just look at characters in this series, we look at the issues they faced, what God told them and how God used them. Through these five men we will look at the covenant, faith, character issues, dealing with the past, relationship with God, the Ten Commandments, feeling inadequate, doing things God's way, getting out of comfort zones, making sure the inside is right, sin and its consequences, and much more.

The whole of the Old Testament is pointing to the New Testament. Many of the Old Testament characters had some of the qualities that Jesus would have had when he came to earth. During this series you might like occasionally to look at how the characters we are looking at, and the stories you'll be reading, point to Jesus.

I hope you enjoy working through this series and I pray that it will help you and your cell draw closer to God.

Cell 1: Abraham - the Covenant

Introduction

Genesis chapters 1-11 are a bit of a disaster for humans; first they eat the fruit, which means sin and death enters the world; then everyone (except Noah and his family) were so wicked (in the bad meaning of the word!) that God wiped them all out with a flood; they then decided to build a tower that would reach the heavens so people would see how great they were. God realised that while they all spoke the same language nothing would be impossible for them. So he dispersed them and made them all speak different languages. This way people would still have to rely on him.

Genesis 12 is a new beginning. It's God's promise and instruction to his people.

God made a covenant with Abraham (then Abram) that he was going to make a great and blessed nation out of him. He blessed Israel, God's chosen nation, so they could bless others.

Christians have a part to play in this (Galatians 3:29). We've been blessed with the truth of the gospel. We're going to have eternal life in heaven. We should be blessing others by telling them.

Cell outline

Ask everyone in your group to think about this question, individually or in pairs: 'What's life all about?' Then get everyone to share with the rest of the group what they think.

Read Genesis 12:2-3. (Before reading it explain to the group that this was a covenant given to Abraham – then Abram – from God and also make sure everyone is aware what covenant means.)

The dictionary definition of covenant is: 1. a solemn agreement; 2. a written promise.

Discuss some of the following questions:

- What does 'blessing' mean? (Make sure you know before you lead this cell.)
- How does God bless people?
- How can we bless others?
- Are we blessing others as we should be? If not, why not?
- Who should we be blessing?

The greatest thing God has ever done to bless people is to send his Son to die for them so that they can have a relationship with him and have eternal life, i.e. THE GOSPEL (John 3:16). Surely this is one of the things we should be blessing other people with? Discuss this as a group. Here are some questions to help you:

- Do people want to hear the gospel? (If not, why not?)
- Do we have the right to share the gospel with people?
- If Jesus was here today how would he share the gospel with people?

Spend some time in prayer. Thank God for the ways he's blessed you and pray for those who aren't as fortunate as you. Perhaps you could find out about a particular country and pray about its needs. Try to keep in touch about what is happening in this country so you can pray for it regularly as a group.

Cell 2: Abraham - faith

Introduction

Hopefully this cell will be a really good one to do if you do not – yet – have Christians in your group. As a group you can discuss why you do or you don't, put your faith in God.

In this cell it would be easy for the Christians to do all the talking and the non-Christians to feel really uncomfortable. Try not to let this happen but encourage them to share their views on faith. For example, get them to share why they have problems putting faith in God.

Also, remember faith is often a major problem for Christians as it is for non-Christians. Everyone goes through doubting stages.

Hopefully this cell will help everyone to understand more about faith.

Read Hebrews 11:11-19. Then use some of the following questions to discuss faith.

Cell outline

What is faith?

The dictionary definition of faith is: 1a. allegiance to duty or a person, loyalty – chiefly in good/bad faith; b. fidelity to one's promises – chiefly in keep/break faith; 2a. belief and trust in and loyalty to God or the doctrines of a religion; b. complete confidence; 3. something believed with strong conviction, especially a system or religious beliefs.

What is the difference between faith and trust?

The dictionary definition of trust is: 1. to place confidence in, rely on; 2. to expect or hope, especially confidently.

- Why do we put faith in some things but not others?
- What kind of evidence do you expect before you put your faith in something? (have examples)
- Why do/don't you put your faith in God?
- Do you feel God has ever let you down? Why?
- What do you struggle with when it comes to faith?
- What happens when we do put our faith in God?
- What do you do when you go through a time of doubting?

- How does your faith compare with Abraham's?
- Why did Abraham have so much faith?

At the end pray about the problems people have with faith.

An extra...

'Instead, they were longing for a better country – a heavenly one' (Hebrews 11:16).

- Do we live as if we're looking forward to heaven?
- Do we make too much of earth when this is really only our temporary residence?
- What are you looking forward to about heaven?

Encourage people to read Genesis 37-45 during the week in preparation for next week's cell on Joseph.

Cell 3: Joseph - character

Introduction

The story of Joseph is probably one of the best known stories in the Bible. Andrew Lloyd Webber even made a hit West End musical out of it. But what makes it so popular?

There are many reasons – Joseph was a man whom God used; he had character, he was an optimist, he made mistakes, but because he never gave up and God's hand was on him, he ended up with one of the top jobs in the world – the Prime Minister of Egypt. He's someone we can relate to and he ended up doing all right.

Joseph is a prime example of how God is with us all the time – he doesn't desert us when we're having a tough time, in fact, he draws even closer to us.

We could spend many weeks looking at Joseph. You might like to do that. However, in this cell we will focus on one main point – character.

Cell outline

Hopefully the people in your group read through the story of Joseph (Genesis 37-45) before you met together. Encourage people to share . . .

> . . . what most struck them about the story.
>
> . . . what part of Joseph's character they could most relate to.
>
> . . . what God taught them by reading the story.
>
> . . . how would you have treated Joseph if he was your step-brother?

It might then be appropriate to pray with each other about what God showed them through the story.

After you have done this (or if you were unable to do this because people hadn't read the story) look at some of the points below.

Brainstorm the good points and the bad points of Joseph's character.

Use some of the following questions:

- How did the 'bad' experiences help Joseph in the long run?
- Has God changed your character (or anything else about you) and how did he do it?
- Can anyone relate to Joseph in the way that God gets us places, but often not the way we would expect?
- Is there anything that you think is hindering God from using you to your full potential? (It might be appropriate to do this in pairs or smaller groups.) After you have shared these things it would be good to pray about them.

Pray together that God would make you into the person he wants you to be.

Encourage people to read Exodus 2-4 in preparation for next week's cell on Moses.

Cell 4: Moses - dealing with the past

Introduction

Moses didn't exactly have the best past in the world. He was a murderer, he had grown up in two different cultures and he had spent the last 40 years being a shepherd in a foreign land. What was more, he was already 80 years old. However, did that stop God using him? No!!

Many of us might feel that we can't be used by God because of our past, whether it is our upbringing or things we have done. However, this is simply not true. God can use us wherever we've come from and whatever we've done. He can even turn around bad stuff in our life to good.

If your cell group are open with each other this could be an excellent cell. It could really give people a chance to let go of the past and move on. However, if your group find it difficult to share, it could be quite tough.

Cell outline

God wants to use us. However, like Moses, we are very good at making excuses. Our past can often be a problem for us, whether we use it as a lame excuse or it is a genuine reason for holding us back.

As a group brainstorm about the excuses Moses made, and some of the excuses you have made.

In twos or threes discuss how our past can hold us back. Why is this the case? If appropriate share back to the rest of the group.

Encourage people to share (if appropriate):
- things from their past that held them back, which they've now overcome.
- things from their past that still hold them back.
- why they think God can't use them (what things they used to think stopped them from being used by God).

How can we overcome our past?

As a group you might want to work through these steps on letting go of the past:

1. Acknowledge there is a problem.

2. Ask for God's forgiveness (if it is something you have done wrong) and know you are forgiven. If it is something someone else has done, you need to forgive them (read 1 Peter 3:18).
3. If you need to make things right with someone – do it.
4. Move on into the future. Romans 12:1-2 (you might want to discuss these verses).
5. Speak to someone about it and be held accountable.

This isn't always a quick process, it can take time, but be patient and keep praying.

Cell 5: Moses - a relationship with God

Introduction

Moses was someone who had an extremely intimate relationship with God. In the passage it tells us about them talking face to face as friends talk (Exodus 33:11).

God wants a close relationship with us. However, do we want this relationship with him? Do we really put in the required effort?

This cell is about our relationship with God. It needs to be adapted so it is useful for the people in your cell. I have just written questions for you to choose the ones you think are the most appropriate to get your group talking.

Cell outline

Read Exodus 33:7-23.

- What strikes you about this passage?

Use some of the following questions:

- Why does God want a relationship with us?
- On a scale of 1-10 (1 being the worst, 10 being the best) how is your relationship with God at the moment?
- Who do you most enjoy spending time with?
- Why do you enjoy spending time with them?
- How much time do you spend with God?
- What could you do that would enable you to enjoy spending time with God as much as others?
- Where do you spend it and what do you do during this time?
- Do you find spending time with God easy? Why?
- Why should we spend time with God?
- What do we get out of it?

We need to spend time with God. The more time we spend with someone the closer we become. You should be longing to spend time with God. The more time we spend with God the more we learn about how he feels about things.

Make each other accountable, set realistic targets of how much time you want to spend with God over the next week.

End this section by praying about the things you have talked about.

WORSHIP: We worship a God who is so holy we would die if we saw his face, in our sinful state. Yet we worship a God who is so merciful he has forgiven us. Read Exodus 33:18-23. Spend some time thinking about it. Then spend some time discussing it as a group, discussing what it means and how it makes you feel. Round up the time with prayer.

Cell 6: Moses - God's standard

Introduction

Moses took the Israelites out of Egypt – they were God's chosen people. However, they weren't much of a nation, they were just a lot of people who had just escaped from slavery.

They needed a structure, a law and legal system. Theirs must have been the best system ever – it came straight from God.

However, many people have a problem with Christianity: they say that there are too many rules and regulations. However, there are a number of problems with this.

1. That's religion, not Christianity. Christianity isn't primarily about rules and regulations. It's about a relationship with God.
2. God created us, he knows how we function best. Therefore, it makes sense to follow these guidelines. It's like getting a manual when you buy something – it helps to read it.

Exodus, Leviticus and Numbers contain many laws but there is one list that is the most famous of all. During this cell we will look at this list – the Ten Commandments.

Cell outline

- Why did God give us the Ten Commandments?
- How do people view the Ten Commandments today?
- Are they still relevant today?

Spend some time looking at some of the Ten Commandments in more detail, pick out those that would most benefit your group. Below is a list of them with some ideas of what you might discuss for each one.

1. You shall have no gods before me.
Who or what controls your life?

2. You shall not make yourselves idols.
Are there any things in your life that could be idols? For example, computer, TV or cars.

3. You shall not misuse the name of the Lord.
Blasphemy is all around us. Have we just come to accept it? If yes, is that right? What should/can we do about it?

4. Remember the Sabbath day and keep it holy.
This is a very, very big issue and you could spend a very long time discussing it. What can we do on Sundays and what shouldn't we do? Should we be doing more to keep Sundays special?

5. Honour your father and mother.
Very hard but very important. Why should we do this? Are there exceptions? Do you do it? How can you do this?

6. You shall not murder.
Read and discuss Matthew 5:21-23. Thought it was an easy one to keep?

7. You shall not commit adultery.
Read and discuss Matthew 5:27-30.

8. You shall not steal.
Stealing from employers – time, phonecalls, stationery.

9. You shall not lie.
Are you honest with yourself, others and God? Have people said things about you that aren't true? Are you still living with these things hanging over you?

What is lying and what isn't? Where do you draw the line?

10. You shall not covet your neighbour's possessions.
In a materialistic society this can be very, very hard. Read and discuss Matthew 6:19-24.

We're never going to achieve God's standards. However, there is hope as God has forgiven us. You might like to spend some time at the end talking about this. Pray that God would help you in the areas you struggle with.

Encourage people to read Judges 6 before next week's cell on Gideon.

Cell 7: Gideon - ever feel inadequate?

Introduction

Gideon wasn't exactly the person you might naturally choose to lead an army against a feared group of warriors. His family was the weakest in the clan and he was the least of his family.

However, it was this that made him an ideal candidate for the job. God chooses to use weak and humble people. Then it is more obvious that it is God who is doing stuff, not just exceptional humans. So do you think God can use you?

This cell should be encouraging. God wants to use normal people. The weaker we feel, the stronger he can make us (2 Corinthians 12:9).

Cell outline

In this cell we will be looking at the part of the story that is recorded in Judges 6. You probably won't want to read all of it, although you might feel this is appropriate. I have recommended a possible section you might like to read. However, it really depends on the people in your cell and whether they know the story of Gideon or not. If they don't, go over an outline of the story in your own words.

Read Judges 6:11-18.
- What was Gideon's reaction when God told him what he wanted him to do?
- What is our reaction when God asks us to do something?
- Why does God use those who feel weak?

We can feel inadequate for many reasons. One reason is because of what people have said about us in the past. Encourage people to share as a group what makes them feel inadequate.

It's often the devil who makes us feel inadequate.
- Why?
- What can we do about feeling inadequate?

The Bible has a lot to say on what we are really like and below is a list. You might want to get each person in your cell to look at one of these and then share their thoughts with the rest of the group.

I AM...

A child of God – Romans 8:16

Forgiven – Colossians 1:13-14

Washed – 1 Corinthians 6:11

Justified – Ephesians 5:1

Born again – 1 Peter 1:24

A new creature – 2 Corinthians 5:17

His workmanship – Ephesians 2:10

A partaker of his divine nature – 2 Peter 1:4

Pure – 1 Peter 1:22

Holy – Hebrews 3:1

A saint – Colossians 1:12

In his hand – John 10:28-29

A son of God – Romans 8:8-14

Strong in the Lord – Ephesians 6:10

Doing all things through Christ who strengthens me – Philippians 4:13

An heir of God and joint heir with Jesus – Romans 8:17

An inheritor of eternal life – 1 John 5:11-12

Blessed with all spiritual blessings – Ephesians 1:3

Healed by his stripes – 1 Peter 2:24

Prosperous – 3 John 2

Above principalities and powers – Ephesians 1:19, 21

More than a conqueror – Romans 8:37

Walking by faith and not by sight – 2 Corinthians 5:7

Being transformed by a renewed mind – Romans 12:1, 2

The righteousness of God in Christ – 2 Corinthians 5:21

Complete in Christ – Colossians 2:9

In the body of Christ – 1 Corinthians 12:12-14

Rooted and grounded in love – Ephesians 3:17

An imitator of Jesus – Ephesians 5:1

The light of the world – Matthew 5:14

Witness

Pray that God would overcome your fear and inadequacies and that he'd give you power and confidence when it comes to sharing your faith.

Encourage people to read Judges 7 before next week's cell.

Cell 8: Gideon - doing things God's way

Introduction

People must have thought Gideon was mad! His army wasn't that big anyway, and then he goes and gets rid of most of them.

So, why did God want Gideon to get rid of his army? Well, he wanted people to realise that he was responsible for delivering his people, not Gideon. The next question that needs to be asked is this: Why did Gideon listen to God? Well, Gideon knew that the only way forward was to trust God.

When God asks us to do something we not only need to do it, but we need to do it his way.

The army provided a little comfort for Gideon and when it was gone he was left vulnerable. However, he had God. We often rely on worldly things to provide us with our comfort. Do we really rely on God?

In this cell we will look at doing things God's way and stepping out of our comfort zones.

Cell outline

Hopefully you managed to get your group to read Judges 7 before you meet together. However, if you didn't, either read it or tell the story in your own words. Then ask some of the following questions.

- Why did God ask Gideon to reduce the size of his army?
- Why did God want to get the credit for this victory?
- Was Gideon sensible to do what God told him to?
- What would have happened if he hadn't reduced the size of his army?
- Has God ever told you to do something in a way that surprised you?

We often want to stay within our comfort zones. One of Gideon's comfort zones was in the number of men he had. However, God got him out of his comfort zone by reducing the size of his army.

- Why do we like comfort zones?
- What would you say your comfort zones are?
- Are there any comfort zones that God has brought you out of in the past?
- Are there any comfort zones you have that you need to get out of?

Discuss this quote: 'Work as if it depended totally on you and pray as if everything depended on God.'

Getting out of our comfort zone when it comes to evangelism is very difficult. Discuss whether as a cell and/or individuals you think you are staying within your comfort zones when it comes to evangelism.

Cell 9: David - inside out

Introduction

God wasn't happy with Saul as king any more, so he told Samuel to go and anoint a new one. The new king was going to be a son of Jesse. When he got there, seven of his sons passed by but God didn't choose any of these. Samuel was confused, so he asked whether there were any more sons. There was: the youngest who was tending the sheep. He was so insignificant that Jesse hadn't even thought of bringing him in from the field for the occasion. But, as seems to be a recurring pattern, God chose him to be the second ever king of his people.

The key verse is 1 Samuel 16:7b '. . . The Lord does not look at the things man looks at. Man looks at the outward appearance, but the Lord looks at the heart.'

Many people these days are very preoccupied about what they look like and what others think about them. But is this useful? What is more important – the inside or the outside?

Cell outline

Read 1 Samuel 16:1-13.

- Are you pleased that God looks on the inside rather than on the outside?
- Do you spend more time worrying about the outside or the inside?
- Are you a 'constant' person or does your personality change when you're with different groups of people?
- Is it a problem if we have different sides to our personality?

It is very easy to stereotype people and put them in a box. These are often preconceived ideas that have little basis in the truth. These are like labels. For example, calling someone a 'square' because they get good marks, or a 'nice person'. These sort of comments can stick and can hurt.

However, snap judgements underpin our everyday lives. We are constantly evaluating, then re-evaluating when we have more information. We need to 'box' people to live – it is what we do with it that counts. We shouldn't trap people in these boxes, they should be able to escape. No one is the same, we are all unique but, at a simple level, boxing is natural. We can get branded as something that we are not. A good reputation can be as harmful as a bad one as you might feel pressure to live up to it. At the end of the day, be yourself, don't let others drag you down.

- What harm can labels/boxes do?
- Can you think of times when you have labelled or boxed people?
- Are there any labels/boxes that people have put on you that you want shifting?

Discuss

- How hard should Christians try to fit in with the rest of society?
- Should we spend lots of money trying to keep up with the latest fashion?

Encourage people to read 2 Samuel 11-12 during the week in preparation for next week's cell.

Cell 10: David - sin, deception and consequences

Introduction

David was extremely successful, but then things started to go wrong. First he committed adultery with Bathsheba, then he tried to solve the problem through deception. When that didn't work he had her husband killed. Although God forgave him for his sin he still had to live with the consequences.

This cell could be very difficult to lead. It will depend on how open your group is. It would be very easy just to talk about things in very general terms. However, you really need to encourage people to share openly and be honest with each other. It will probably be worth doing some of this cell in smaller groups.

Cell outline

It would be good to get people to share things that have happened in their own life. For example, a time they have sinned and what happened. People can learn from experiences of others in the cell so perhaps they won't make the same mistakes too.

Hopefully, people would have read the passage beforehand. Encourage people to share what they learnt from the passage and how they thought it related to their life.

- After David had sinned, what should he have done?
- What should we do after we have sinned?
- God wanted David to be king, He had plans for his life so why did he allow him to sin?
- If God forgives us why do we have to suffer the consequences? Why doesn't God just remove them too?

As a group talk about escape routes for sin. (For example, if you struggle with what you see on television, channel flicking late at night is not a very good idea.)

Explaining the gospel to people is not easy. However, it gets even more difficult when you have to explain that although God forgives us our sin we still often have to live with the consequences. How would you explain why this is to others?

The basic problem that got David into this mess was lust. Discuss the problem of lust. (It would probably be best to do this in single sex groups.)
- What is the problem with lust?
- What should we do with lust?
- How should we deal with it?

Be accountable.

You could finish this cell by playing some music and getting people to spend some time alone with God. Get them to ask God if they have any unresolved sin in their life and what they're meant to do with it. In might be then appropriate to split into twos or threes to pray about this and hold each other accountable.

JESUS

Introduction

Jesus has had more impact on the world than any other person in its history. Jesus' birth was seen as so significant that its date has become the reference point for our calendar. In modern terms Jesus didn't really influence that many people during his short time on earth. However, his ministry has lived on like no other person in history. So who is this Jesus? What is all the fuss about?

The answer can be found in the book where so much is written about him – the Bible. The Bible has two parts, many describe them as a question section and an answer section. The Old Testament contains the questions, the New Testament the answers. Jesus is that answer. The Old Testament all points to Jesus, it shows us why Jesus needed to come and what he would be like when he did come. The New Testament presents Jesus and explains what happens now the answer has come.

So if Jesus is the answer, it's important that we take time learning about him. The word Christian simply means 'little Christ', therefore as Christians we need to be like Jesus (Christ is another name used for Jesus). We need to know what he was like and how he acted. How did Jesus relate to his father? How did Jesus mix with sinners? How did Jesus relate to people? What was Jesus' reaction to sin? One of the aims of this series is to make Jesus our role model.

This series is by no means comprehensive, it only scratches the surface of Jesus' life and ministry. It's just a brief overview. However, I hope that it gets people intrigued and excited about him. Over the years many Churches seemed to have taken the excitement and the charisma out of Jesus. They've watered him down. Is the picture of a meek and mild Jesus, wearing perfectly clean clothes, with a perfect face, beautiful hair and a glow that follows him around really true? Judge for yourself!

Cell 1: Jesus - in the Old Testament

Introduction

As Jesus is the centre of our faith it might seem reasonable that we only read the part of the Bible that is about him. Therefore many people end up just reading the New Testament, hardly ever touching the Old Testament. There are many problems with this approach. One is that the Old Testament is actually about Jesus – it is constantly referring to him and pointing to him.

This cell is an introduction to the series on Jesus. In it we will look at what the Old Testament says about him.

Cell outline

Split the cell into groups of twos or threes and then give each group one or two of the following passages. Get each group to read them and think about them. After a while come back together as a whole group and share with each other the passages and what they say about Jesus. Brainstorm on a piece of paper what these passages say Jesus is going to be like.

Psalm 72:12-14	Isaiah 42:1-4	Daniel 7:13-14, 27
Isaiah 6:9-10	Isaiah 53	Micah 5: 2, 4-5
Isaiah 9:1-2, 6-7	Isaiah 61:1-2	Zechariah 9:9
Isaiah 11:1-5	Jeremiah 23:5-8	

Portraits of Jesus

The characters of the Old Testament also point to Jesus. Many of them have some of the qualities that Jesus would later have. Of course they were all only human so had their faults, whereas Jesus was the perfect Son of God. Summarise the story and explanation below to your group. Then brainstorm on a large piece of paper the qualities of some of the characters in the Old Testament who point to Jesus. For example, David became a king, but he started as a humble shepherd.

- What characteristics of Jesus do you see in yourself/others in your cell?
- How do you want to become more like Jesus this week? Pray with each other that you will be able to do this.

Finish this section by thanking God for Jesus. Be creative!!

I have been told that somewhere in Russia there is a palace containing a famous 'Hall of Beauty.' In this room are hung more than 850 portraits of young women painted by Count Rotari for Empress Catherine the second. The artist journeyed through all the 50 provinces of Russia to find his models. It is said, however, that when he had finished, the 850 portraits bore an unusual resemblance to Catherine the Second, either by some gesture, pose, facial characteristic, jewel, flower, dress, or occupation, there was a delicate reference to the empress.

The story is an example of the way we attempt to flatter other human beings. But it is also an apt illustration of one way in which God has revealed Jesus Christ to us in his Word. Those who have been called by God, whose stories have been told in the Scriptures – men like Abraham, Moses and David – are in one sense God's pictures. They are painted by him through his grace, and in them some of the characteristics of Jesus Christ may be seen. We ought now to turn from the portraits to the One who is himself altogether lovely and for whom and by whom they were commissioned.

James Montgomery Boice
Ordinary Men Called by God

Cell 2: Jesus - fact or fiction

Introduction

His birth was so important that the world marks time by it. We celebrate it every year. Most people have a picture of what Jesus' birth was like. But was it really like that? Was Jesus' birth anything like how it's portrayed on the Christmas cards we give and receive each year? When you think of Christmas, what is the first thing you think of? Is it Jesus being born in a dirty, smelly manger? Is it your Christmas dinner or opening presents under the tree? Is it the King of the universe being visited by shepherds? Is it the wise men travelling for years to see the child? Do you ever give a thought to his mum and dad?

In this cell we will try to begin to discover what the first Christmas might have been like.

Cell outline

Icebreaker ideas

It would be good to start off the Christmas theme with an icebreaker. You could ask people one of the following questions:

- What does Christmas mean to you?
- What is the best part of Christmas?
- How would you spend your perfect Christmas day?
- What is the first thing you think about when you think of Christmas?

The Christmas myth

Discuss as a group how we envisage the first Christmas. Try to get some old Christmas cards to give you ideas. Brainstorm on a large piece of paper what the group make the first Christmas out to be like.

You could also discuss what Christmas has become in this country at the beginning of the twenty-first century.

The real first Christmas

Split up into groups of two or three. Look at the first Christmas from a particular angle. Use the accounts of the first Christmas in the Gospels to help you do this. These are some of the possible angles you could look at it from:

- Mary and Joseph
- The families of Mary and Joseph

- The shepherds
- The wise men
- Herod
- The conditions Jesus was born into compared to a king of that time.

Once you have looked at the first Christmas from different angles, feed back to the rest of the group what you think it was like. Then as a whole group discuss why it was like this. Why did Jesus have to be born in this way?

Worship ideas

After looking at how and why Jesus was born, turn to worship God for his incredible gift. You could use John 3:16 as the basis for this time of worship.

Cell 3: Jesus - fact or fiction?

Introduction

This cell will give you a chance to debate whether you think Jesus actually existed or not, and if he did exist, whether he rose from the dead or not.

If you have non-Christians in your cell it will give you a chance to discuss why you believe what you believe and the reasoning behind it. If everyone in your cell is a Christian it is still a useful exercise, as it will give you a chance to look at both sides of the argument and practise how to respond to those who don't believe Jesus existed and/or rose from the dead.

Cell outline

In this cell split into three groups, each taking one of the three points of view stated below. Give everyone 10-15 minutes in their groups to prepare their arguments. Get each group to appoint a spokesperson who will have three minutes to present their case. They can call on one 'witness' whom they can question. (For example, the group arguing that Jesus did rise from the dead might want to call up Mary Magdalene or Thomas.) After all three cases have been presented, the other groups can question them.

Here are the three different sides to the argument:
1. Jesus never existed.

2. Jesus existed, he did and said many good things, then he was killed on a cross, died and that was the end of it.

3. Jesus is exactly as the Bible says. He was born to a virgin, lived a perfect life, died and rose again.

It would depend on what happens during the debate as to how you end this cell. You could finish by reading a passage (for example, 1 Peter 2:22-25), then give people a chance to spend some time thinking in silence. End by either playing some music and/or having a time of open prayer.

Icebreaker idea

You could do a 'Fact or Fiction' quiz. Split the cell into teams and ask them a series of questions that are either 'True' or 'False'.

Cell 4: Jesus - Son of God, Son of Man, King and Servant

Introduction

Jesus the Son of God came down to earth and was born to human parents. So as well as being the pure, holy and perfect Son of God, he also became a Son of Man. He was brought up as any child would have been in those days. When he was old enough he learnt his father's trade – carpentry. In many senses Jesus, the Son of God, led a fairly ordinary life for the first 30 years. But have you ever really thought what it must have been like? When did Jesus realise that he wasn't just a normal child, that he was actually the Son of God? Imagine what it must have been like for him knowing that he was on this earth to die for our sins.

Jesus was a king, he is king of the universe, he is the central figure of the Christian faith, he is the most remarkable person who has ever lived. But despite all this he had the attitude of a servant.

In this cell we will look at Jesus' attitude and think about how he lived as the Son of God and as a Son of Man. We will look at the fact that although he was a king he lived as a servant. With his life in mind we will think about how we should live our life.

Cell outline

Brainstorm on a large piece of paper everything Jesus was like when he lived on earth. For example, King, Son of God, Human, Servant and Perfect.

Read Philippians 2:5-11.

Spend some time in silence or with some music playing in the background, thinking about the life of Jesus. Think about his dual nature – Son of God/Son of Man, King/Servant. Try to imagine what it must have been like for him living on earth among normal people, knowing everything he knew. Think how hard it must have been to have that servant attitude.

Then discuss as a group what you were thinking about during the silence.

In verse 5 it says 'Your attitude should be the same as that of Christ Jesus . . .' Spend some time either as individuals or in twos/threes thinking about what this means and how you should be living your life. Then come back as a whole group and feed back what you have been discussing.

The Bible has much to say about having a servant attitude. In twos or threes look at some of the following passages, then come back together as a whole group and discuss what you have found out.

Jesus instructs people to be servants
Mark 9:33-37 Luke 22:27 John 13:12-17

Marks of a servant
Philippians 2:4 Galatians 6:2 Matthew 6:33
1 Corinthians 4:7 2 Corinthians 10:17 Ephesians 4:2

Servants can only serve one master
Luke 16:13 Matthew 6:24 1 Corinthians 4:1

The rewards for being a servant
1 Corinthians 4:2 Matthew 25:31-40 2 Timothy 2:4
Matthew 25:21

You might like to use some of the following questions to start the discussion and to keep it moving:
- Jesus was a servant. What were some of the things he did as a servant?
- What are some of the characteristics of a servant attitude?
- Think of some of the practical ways we could put this servant attitude into action?
- What do you find easy/hard about having a servant attitude?

Conclude this cell by praying for each other that you would be able to have a servant attitude like Jesus. Before you pray, ask people if there are any particular issues they would like prayer for, related to this topic.

Cell 5: Jesus - living in the world

Introduction

As Christians we are told to live in the world but not be of the world (John 15:19). It's a very hard thing to do. There are so many questions that surround this: How different should we be? How much can we fit in? Should we spend time with non-Christians?

Jesus lived a perfect life in this world for over 30 years, so I think he must be a very good person to use as our role model when we consider how to live in the world but not be of the world. So in this cell we will look at what Jesus did and said about this matter.

Cell outline

Read and discuss Matthew 9:9-13 using the questions below to stimulate discussion if necessary.

- What does this passage mean?
- What has this got to do with us?
- Following Jesus' example, how should we act?
- Are there places where, as Christians, we should not go?

Living in the world is hard. Discuss with each other, either as a whole group or in smaller groups, what you find particularly difficult. If issues come up try to help each other to decide what is right or wrong. Point each other to relevant verses in the Bible. As a cell leader prepare for this by finding passages in the Bible relating to things you think are likely to come up.

Read and discuss Jude 23.
Make sure you have read through the box on the right before the cell. You might like to use parts of it during the discussion.

At the end of the cell split up into twos or threes and pray for each other. Hold each other accountable.

About Jude 23

This verse is all about evangelism. We are called to go into the fire (the world) and snatch others out of it (non-Christians). We are on a rescue mission.

When we go into the fire to snatch others from it we must be careful as we don't want to get burnt (caught up and attracted to the sin of the world) ourselves. Once something has caught fire it is quickly devoured (once we are caught up in the world's way of doing things it's hard to escape). So before we go into the fire we must be prepared.

Firefighters receive lots of training before they try to rescue people from fires. We need to do the same. Firefighters also make sure they wear their protective clothing. The armour of God is our protective clothing and you can read about it in Ephesians 6:10-20. Cell can be a training ground where you can learn from each other how to survive the flames. You can pray for each other and hold each other accountable so you don't get caught up.

We have got to hate sin. We must love the sinner but hate the sin. It puts it very strongly in this verse, '. . . hating even the clothing stained by corrupted flesh.' But, do we hate sin? Do we really hate things that are slightly contaminated by sin? Or do we actually find sin quite attractive and appealing? In a future cell we will look at Jesus' reaction to sin, but in the meantime ask God to help you and teach you how to hate sin.

Cell 6: Jesus - reaction to sin

Introduction

While Jesus was living on earth he never sinned. However, like us, he spent a lot of time with people who did. So what was his reaction to sin? In this cell we will look at two passages in the New Testament that are two examples of how Jesus reacted to sin. We will first look at how he acted towards sin, then we will look at how we should react to it.

Remember you might either have to define the word sin carefully at the beginning of your cell or use a different word altogether.

Cell outline

Read Matthew 21:12-13 and discuss using some of the following questions:

- Why did Jesus get so angry?
- Why might he have reacted as he did?
- Does sin make you angry?
- What sins in particular make you angry?
- Do you think it is a problem if sin doesn't make us angry. Should it?
- Following Jesus' example, how should we react to sin?

(Remember there's a difference between anger and righteous anger)

Read John 8:2-11 and discuss using some of the following questions:

- How would you have reacted in this (or similar) situations?
- What did Jesus' reaction show the teachers of the Law and the Pharisees?
- What did Jesus' reaction show the women?
- When Jesus wrote something on the ground, what do you think he was writing?
- Looking at this example, how should we react to sinners?

Discuss the statement 'Hate the sin, love the sinner'. What does it mean? Do we do it? How should we do it?

One of the cell values is 'Belong before you believe before you behave'. Spend some time discussing this as a group. Does this happen in your cell? How can you make sure it happens?

At the end of this cell spend some time in silence (or with some quiet music) so people can reflect on their own lives (perhaps use Matthew 7:1-5 as the basis for this time). Afterwards, in small groups, pray, encourage and hold each other accountable.

Cell 7: Jesus - his commands

Introduction

The Pharisees and teachers of the Law were often trying to trick Jesus, hoping that he would eventually say something that was in total contradiction to the Law as it appears in the Old Testament.

This account in Luke is just another of these attempts. However, Jesus tells the Pharisee to read from 'the Law' and, as ever, Jesus and the Law are in total agreement.

Cell outline

As always, this cell needs to be flexible. Below are just a few ideas on how you can get your cell to think about these two commands. How you do it is up to you.

A possible icebreaker idea would be to get the group to make up a sketch based on the story of the Good Samaritan, perhaps as a modern day version.

Read and discuss Luke 10:25-28.

- What are the two commands of Jesus?
- How are they linked?
- How did Jesus live out these commands?
- How can we live out these commands?
- Do you find it easy or hard to live these commands and why?

Read Luke 10:29-37, then either discuss it or you could have some silence first where people can reflect on the story and think about some of the questions below before discussing them.

- Which person in the story can you most relate to at the moment and why?
- What does the story tell us about what we should be like?
- Did reading and thinking about this story challenge you in any way today? If so, why and how are you going to change because of it?

At the end of this section spend some time praying about what you have read and discussed. Pray for each other as you seek to live out the commands of Christ.

Cell 8: Jesus - his teaching

Introduction

You could spend every cell group until the day you die looking at the teaching of Jesus and still not do it justice. So why are we even bothering to look at it in just one cell meeting?

This cell isn't really about looking at the content of Jesus' teaching. (If you want to do that use 'Blueprint for Life', which looks at his teaching in the Sermon on the Mount.) In this cell we will look at a variety of his teachings and see how radical and counter-cultural they were.

Cell outline

Split into groups of two or three. Then give each group one of the following passages to look at. Before the cell it is important that you read all these passages and make sure you understand them. (You could go through them with your cell supervisor.) Choose carefully which passages to look at; select ones you think will be most relevant for your group.

- The Beatitudes — Matthew 5:1-12

- Lord of the Sabbath — Matthew 12:1-14
  Mark 2:23-3:6
  Luke 6:1-11

- The rich young man — Matthew 19:16-30
  Mark 10:17-31

- The widow's offering — Mark 12:41-44
  Luke 21:1-4

- Love for enemies — Matthew 5:43-48
  Luke 6:27-36

- Jesus questioned about fasting — Matthew 9:14-17
  Mark 2:18-22
  Luke 5:33-39

- The cost of being a disciple — Luke 14:25-35

- The shepherd and his flock — John 10:1-21

- The world hates the disciples   John 15:18-16:4
- The parable of the shrewd manager   Luke 16:1-15
- The parable of the workers in the vineyard   Matthew 20:1-16

Get each group to discuss the following questions about the passages:
- What was Jesus teaching his audience?
- Did it go against the grain of the culture at the time? Why?
- What were people's reactions to his teaching?
- How is this teaching relevant for us?
- How would the world react to Jesus' teaching today?

Spend plenty of time doing this. Then get all the groups to share with the whole cell what they found out about Jesus' teaching from their passage(s).

To end, read John 6:60-69 and discuss how you are going to react to Jesus' teaching:
- Are you going to ignore it, or act on it?
- If you are going to act on it, what will you have to change and how will your life change as a result?
- Do you need to learn more about what Jesus taught? If yes, how are you going to go about doing this?
- Are you going to keep Jesus' teaching to yourself or are you going to share it with others? If yes, who are you going to share it with and how?

You could spend some time in silence thinking about these things before you discuss them as a group. After you have spent some time discussing the questions and passage, split up into small groups and pray for each other.

Cell 9: Jesus - his death

Introduction

Jesus' death and resurrection was the climax of his ministry on earth. He was the perfect Son of God. He died so that we might be forgiven and have a relationship with God, his Father.

In this cell we will begin by looking at why Jesus died. We will then look at the story of the crucifixion, the resurrection and the run up to these events, thinking about everything Jesus went through for us. Then we will turn these thoughts into worship, thanking him for all he has done.

Cell outline

Read John 3:16-21. Discuss the following questions:

- Why did God send Jesus into the world?
- It would have been easy for Jesus to condemn the world. He didn't – what did he do instead? Think of examples where he could have condemned but didn't.
- Why did so many people have such a problem with Jesus?

Read Romans 6:23 and discuss:

- Why did Jesus have to die for our sins? Couldn't God have provided another way for us to be forgiven and have a relationship with him?

Split up into four groups. Get each group to look at one of the following passages and, using the Gospel accounts, begin to get a picture of what Jesus must have been thinking.

- *During his life as he began to predict his death to his disciples.*
  (Matthew 16:21-28, 17:17-19; Mark 10:32-34; Luke 18:31-34; John 12:20-36)
- *During the last supper and the time leading up to his arrest.*
  (Matthew 26:17-56; Mark 14:12-52; Luke 22:7-53; John 13)
- *During the trials.*
  (Matthew 26:57-68, 27:11-31; Mark 14:53-65, 15:1-20; Luke 22:63-23:25; John 18:2-14, 19-24, 28-40, 19:1-16)
- *On the cross.*
  (Matthew 27:32-56; Mark 15:21-41; Luke 23:26-49; John 19:17-37)

Then come back as a group and share your thoughts about how Jesus must have been feeling.

Spend some time worshipping and thanking God for sending his Son and letting him die for our sins. Be creative!

Cell 10: Jesus - our response

Introduction

During this series you have hopefully learnt a lot about the character of Jesus. As Christians we are meant to be followers of Christ. In fact, the word Christian means 'little Christ'. We are meant to live our lives trying to be as much like Jesus as we can.

This cell concludes the series on Jesus and encourages people to make a response to what they have learnt. This cell needs to be left fairly flexible. What you do in this cell will depend greatly on what has happened in the nine cells before this one. Below are some ideas of what you could do to conclude this series.

Cell outline

Brainstorm on a piece of paper as many things as possible that you have learnt about Jesus during this series. After you have done this you might like to ask your group to consider and share with the rest of the group some of the following:

- What characteristic of Jesus most impacted on you and why?
- What characteristic of Jesus did you find the most surprising?
- What characteristic of Jesus do you think is most evident in your own life?
- What characteristic of Jesus would you like to see more in your own life? (How are you going to go about seeing that this happens?)
- How would you describe Jesus to someone who had never heard of him before? (You could get everyone in the group to write a paragraph individually then encourage them to read them out to the rest of the group.)

In the Gospels people have many different responses to Jesus. We will now look at some of them. Split the group into smaller groups and give each a few of the passages below. After they have had a chance to read and discuss them, encourage them to feed back to the large group a brief description of the response and why they think the person responded in that way.

- Matthew 2:13-16
- Matthew 3:13-14
- Matthew 26:14-16
- Matthew 27:39-40
- Mark 1:16-20

JESUS: CELL 10

- Mark 5:27-34
- Mark 10:21-22
- Mark 14:66-72
- Mark 15:16-20
- Luke 5:27-29
- Luke 10:38-42
- Luke 17:11-19
- John 4:28-30
- John 6:60-69

Now spend some time individually thinking about what their response to Jesus is.

Then split into small groups again and encourage people to share what they have learnt, what they want to change in their own lives and what they want their response to be. Then pray with each other.